A M E R I C A N   T R A I L S

⊛

TRAILS TO THE WEST
Beyond the Mississippi

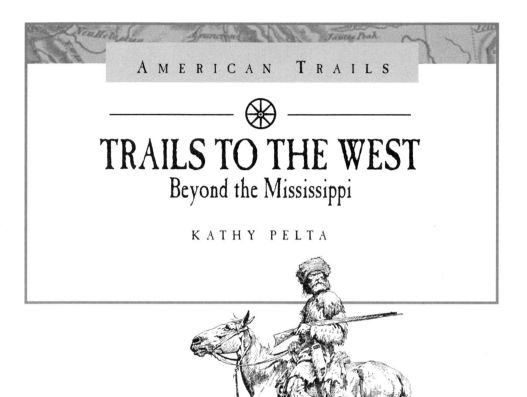

AMERICAN TRAILS

TRAILS TO THE WEST
Beyond the Mississippi

KATHY PELTA

RSVP
RAINTREE
STECK-VAUGHN
PUBLISHERS
The Steck-Vaughn Company

Austin, Texas

Published by Raintree Steck-Vaughn Publishers, an imprint of Steck-Vaughn Company

Raintree Steck-Vaughn Publishers Staff
Publishing Director: Walter Kossmann   Project Manager: Lyda Guz
Editor: Shirley Shalit   Electronic Production: Scott Melcer
Photo Editor: Margie Foster

Library of Congress Cataloging-in-Publication Data
Pelta, Kathy.
    Trails to the West : beyond the Mississippi / by Kathy Pelta.
        p.   cm.– (American trails)
    Includes bibliographical references (p.   ) and index.
    Summary: Describes the hardships and accomplishments of the different groups who established the various trails used to travel westward across the United States in the mid-1800s.
    ISBN 0-8172-4072-1
    1. Frontier and pioneer life – West (U.S.) – Juvenile literature.   2. Trails – West (U.S.) – History – Juvenile literature.   3. West (U.S.) – History – Juvenile literature.
    [1. Trails – West (U.S.)   2. Frontier and pioneer life – West (U.S.)   3. West (U.S.) – History – 1848–1860.]   I. Title.   II. Series: Pelta, Kathy. American trails.
F590.5.P45   1997
978 – dc21   96-39483
                                                                              CIP   AC
Printed and bound in the United States
1 2 3 4 5 6 7 8 9 0 LB 00 99 98 97

Acknowledgments
Cover (inset) © Superstock, (map) The Granger Collection; p. 3 North Wind Picture Archive; p. 6 The Granger Collection; p. 7 © Superstock; p. 10 The Granger Collection; pp. 11, 12 North Wind Picture Archive; p. 14 © Superstock; pp. 16, 18 North Wind Picture Archive; p. 19 © Superstock; p. 23 (top) Colorado Historical Society, (bottom) © Joe Bator/The Stock Market; p. 26 The Granger Collection; p. 28 © Superstock; pp. 29 (both), 31 North Wind Picture Archive; p. 34 © Church of Jesus Christ of Latter Day Saints; p. 38 Frederic Remington Art Museum, Ogdensburg, NY; p. 40 The Granger Collection; p. 41 © Galen Rowell; p. 42 © Superstock; p. 47 © Superstock; p. 48 Oregon Historical Society; p. 49 © Pete Saloutos/The Stock Market; p. 52 North Wind Picture Archive; p. 53 The Granger Collection; pp. 55-56 © Superstock; p. 60 North Wind Picture Archive; pp. 61, 64, 65 The Granger Collection; pp. 66, 68 North Wind Picture Archive; p. 70 © Superstock; p. 75 LA County Natural History Museum; p. 77 © Galen Rowell; p. 78 The Granger Collection; p. 79 North Wind Picture Archive; p. 81 Brown Brothers; p. 82 © Corbis; p. 84 Brown Brothers; p. 85 North Wind Picture Archive.

Cartographer: Geo Systems, Inc.

Contents

North American Trails

There were trails winding through the woods and wilderness of North America long before any Europeans arrived. Some paths were shortcuts that animals took to salt licks, or to favorite water holes. Native Americans used these paths or created their own as they hunted and gathered food, traded with neighbors, and made pilgrimages to sacred sites.

The first Europeans to explore North America usually followed established trails. Sometimes, with the help of native guides, they blazed new ones. After the explorers came soldiers and missionaries, traders and trappers, settlers, and eventually cattle ranchers moving their herds to market. Gradually, some of the most-used trails all across

Many emigrants, such as these crossing what is Arkansas today, traveled beyond the Mississippi to set up homesteads.

the country were widened to accommodate oxcarts and horse-drawn wagons, then stagecoaches, and finally, motorcars. Some trails became routes for railroad lines.

The trails that crisscrossed the country reflected its history. In the 1500s, Spain claimed much of what is now the United States. In the Southeast, the Southwest, and along the coast of what is now California, Spanish trails linked missions, military posts, and towns.

By the 1600s, people from England and some other countries of Europe had settled on North America's eastern shores. They, too, established trails as they moved inland. By 1763, England claimed lands as far west as the Mississippi River. Until long after the English colonies became the United States, the frontier of the East remained at the Mississippi.

Typical of many westward travelers was this prospector seeking minerals in the open country.

By the early 1800s, some explorers, trappers, fur traders, and missionaries had crossed the Mississippi to venture farther west. As farmland became scarce in the east, more people chose to cross the river and move on. In the mid-1800s, the "Great Western Migration" was on as Americans by the thousands went west. They followed many different routes—the Oregon Trail, the California Trail, the Mormon Trail, the Santa Fe and Gila Trails, or a traders' and trappers' trail known as the Old Spanish Trail. These westbound travelers included adventurers, prospectors, religious groups, and homesteaders seeking better lives for their families. This is their story.

The Opening Wedge

I n 1792, only nine years after the Americans gained their independence from Great Britain, Captain Robert Gray sailed from Boston in his ship, *Columbia*, on a trading expedition. After rounding the tip of South America, Gray sailed up the western coast of North America and into the mouth of a great river. He named it the Columbia, after his ship.

Because of Captain Gray's discovery, the United States claimed the territory people called "the Oregon Country," an area much larger than today's state of Oregon. The Oregon Country included most of the present states of Oregon, Washington, and Idaho, parts of Nevada, Utah, and Wyoming, and the southwestern corner of Canada.

Farther north, at nearly the same time as Gray's voyage, a Scottish fur trader named Alexander Mackenzie crossed west over the Canadian Rocky Mountains to reach Canada's Pacific Coast. On the basis of Mackenzie's overland trek, Great Britain also claimed the Oregon Country.

Eleven years later, in 1803, President Thomas Jefferson bought from France a vast, unexplored region called Louisiana. This land extended from the Mississippi River west to the Rocky Mountains, nearly doubling the size of the United States. In addition to what is now the state of

Louisiana, the Louisiana Purchase included all or parts of what are now the states of Arkansas, Missouri, Iowa, Nebraska, North and South Dakota, Minnesota, Oklahoma, Kansas, Colorado, Wyoming, and Montana.

Immediately President Jefferson sent Captain Meriwether Lewis and Lieutenant William Clark to explore this unknown land. Their expedition included 26 soldiers, hunters, and interpreters. In May 1804, the men set out by boat from their camp on the Missouri River, just upstream from the bustling Mississippi River port of St. Louis. The men planned to follow the Missouri west and north to its source somewhere in the Rocky Mountains. An important goal of the Lewis and Clark expedition was to find a river

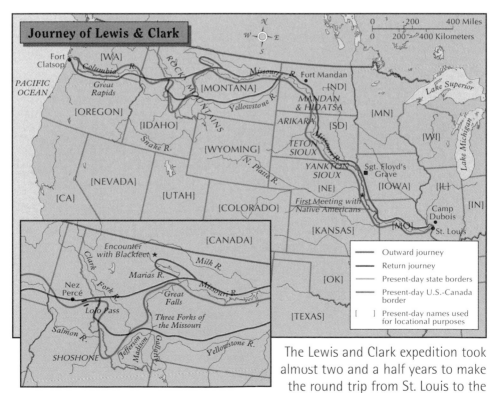

The Lewis and Clark expedition took almost two and a half years to make the round trip from St. Louis to the Pacific coast in Oregon.

In this artist's rendition, Sacagawea points out something in the distance to Lewis (center) and Clark.

that flowed into the mighty Columbia River. Since European explorers in North America had first realized the enormous width of the continent, it had been their dream to find this "Northwest Passage."

As Lewis and Clark began their journey west, they were unsure what lay ahead. Although the two had brought along Alexander Mackenzie's book about his westward trek to the Pacific in 1793, it contained no useful maps. And besides, the Scottish explorer had crossed the Canadian Rockies, to the north. This expedition intended to cross the Rocky Mountains much farther south.

By the following summer, Lewis and Clark had ventured into the Oregon Country, beyond the Rocky Mountains and the western boundary of the Louisiana Purchase territory. Part of the way, a Shoshone Indian woman, Sacagawea, had helped to guide them. In late winter they reached the Pacific Ocean—but without finding a waterway linking the Missouri and Columbia Rivers.

In the spring of 1806, the expedition started back to St. Louis. Passing through what is now North Dakota, the men met two fur trappers who had come up the Missouri River in search of beaver, following the same route Lewis and Clark took when they headed west two years before. John Colter, a hunter with the expedition, wanted to try his hand at trapping, too, and asked Lewis and Clark for permission to remain in the wilderness. The two leaders agreed, and gave Colter parting gifts they hoped he would find useful—a gun and some powder and lead for making bullets.

Once Lewis and Clark returned to St. Louis, they began work on the official report of their findings. The writing took longer than expected, and in 1807—before they could publish their report—Patrick Gass, a sergeant with the expedition, published his diary. An unknown artist illustrated the booklet with engravings (hand-drawn pictures that were carved on a metal plate and then printed). Americans were fascinated by Sergeant Gass's account with such colorful illustrations as "Captains Lewis & Clark holding a Council with the Indians," "Captain Clark & his men building a line of Huts," "Captain Lewis shooting an Indian," "A Canoe striking on a Tree," and "Captain Clark and his men shooting Bears."

This picture in Patrick Gass's book shows Lewis and Clark meeting Native Americans at Council Bluffs, in today's Iowa.

By the time Gass's diary was published, merchant ships from Boston were making regular stops along the coast of the Pacific Northwest to trade manufactured goods for the Native Americans' sea otter skins, and then sailing on to China to trade the furs for tea, fine china dishes, and Chinese silks. From the sea captains' stories, people in the eastern United States were learning much about the coast of the Oregon Country. Now, from the stories of Sergeant Gass, the easterners had a glimpse of what life in the western wilderness must be like.

John Colter, meanwhile, was learning firsthand about life in the Far West. After leaving the Lewis and Clark expedition, Colter had stayed only a short time with the two trappers before setting out on his own. As he looked for beaver, Colter explored on foot nearly every river and canyon and mountain pass in what are now the states of Wyoming, Montana, and Idaho. Colter was the first of the mountain men—the small band of hardy woodsmen who in their hunt for furs were to spread out over the entire Rocky Mountain region in the next 30 years.

Like John Colter, the mountain men who came after usually worked alone or in small groups. Constantly on the move in search of beaver, they kept to remote areas as they followed each stream to its source. In their wanderings, these trappers established trails that helped to push the American frontier far to the west.

In this illustration, artist Frederic Remington shows an old-time mountain man with his ponies.

ONE

✵

Early Trailblazers in the Rockies

Before the 1800s, the users of western trails were mainly Native Americans carrying furs, shells, arrowheads, or other items to trade. Scattered among them were a few European fur trappers—mainly French. After Lewis and Clark returned to report on the huge number of beaver along the upper Missouri River, many American trappers rushed west to make their fortunes. For there was a growing demand for the soft beaver furs, or "plews," to trim ladies' stylish garments, and to produce felt to make the gentlemen's tall hats that were all the rage in the cities of Europe.

One of the first Americans to go west in search of beaver was Manuel Lisa, a businessman from St. Louis. Lisa's plan was to set up posts along the upper Missouri River to trade with the Native Americans. In 1810 he started upriver with a boatload of 42 trappers and a guide, a part-French Canadian and part-Shawnee man named George Drouillard who had been a scout with the Lewis and Clark expedition. Lisa followed the Missouri River as far north as the present border between North Dakota and Montana. From there he went down the Yellowstone River to its junction with the Bighorn River in what is now central Montana. Here the men built a fort they called Manuel's Fort. Then they fanned out in all directions to hunt beaver.

13

Trapping for furs was not Manuel Lisa's only aim. He also wanted his men to make friends with the Native Americans, and set up trade alliances with all of the native groups in the area. By doing this, he hoped to establish a monopoly on the fur trade in the upper Missouri River area. Manual Lisa did make friends with the Crows and the Flatheads—only to discover that by agreeing to trade with them he had lost his chance to trade, or even be friends, with their traditional enemies, the Blackfeet.

Around this time John Colter appeared at Manuel's Fort. Since leaving the Lewis and Clark expedition in 1806 to trap, Colter had grown familiar with this part of the northern Rockies. For a while, he joined Lisa's group as a trapper. At the same time, he did more exploring—as always, alone. On one trip, Colter crossed the Bighorn and Teton Mountains to discover Jackson Hole in what is now Grand Teton National Park in northwestern Wyoming. On another journey, he prowled through what is now Yellowstone National Park, where he came upon Yellowstone Lake and spouting geysers.

Geysers, such as the Castle Geyser shown here, were undoubtedly seen by John Colter when he visited the Yellowstone region.

While Manuel Lisa worked toward his goal of securing a monopoly on fur trade on the upper Missouri, another American was trying to do the same in the Pacific Northwest. In 1810, German-born John Jacob Astor, who had already made a fortune in the fur trade in the east, formed the Pacific Fur Company and made plans to start a trading post, to be called Astoria, at the mouth of the Columbia River. The following year, Wilson Price Hunt and several other company men left St. Louis to attempt an overland journey to Astoria. Marie Dorian, wife of Pierre Dorian, guide and interpreter for Wilson Price Hunt, accompanied her husband on his 1811 overland expedition to Astoria. During the journey Marie, who also brought along her two young children, gave birth to a third child. Despite this event and several near-disasters, the group finally reached Astoria.

A few months later, Robert Stuart and a half-dozen other Astoria agents made a return trip to St. Louis. They took a boat up the Columbia River, and then, to cross the Cascade Mountains, bought horses from a group of Native Americans. In the dry, sandy region east of the Cascades, rattlesnakes were a constant problem. Hoping to keep the snakes away when they camped at night, the men sprinkled tobacco around their tents.

Although Stuart wisely avoided Hell's Canyon on the Snake River, he still found it hard-going along the valley of the Snake in what is now southern Idaho. To avoid trouble with the Crow Indians, Stuart led his men on a wide detour to the north. Crossing the Tetons, the group met some Crows who told him of a pass through the mountains to the Platte River. Stuart followed the Indian trail to the pass, later called the South Pass. He found it so broad and gently sloping that crossing over was no problem. Once out of the mountains, Stuart and the others followed the Platte and Missouri Rivers to the Mississippi.

The route Stuart followed was almost the same as the one that later became the Oregon Trail. And years later, the 20-mile-wide South Pass made it possible for emigrants to bring their wagons over the mountains on their way to California and the Oregon Country. These early west-bound travelers were called "emigrants" because they were leaving the United States for foreign territories—California, which still belonged to Mexico, and the Oregon Country which was jointly held by Great Britain and the United States according to a treaty that was first signed in 1818 and renewed twice after that.

In 1822, just ten years after Robert Stuart's west-to-east crossing of the Rockies, and at almost the same time the Santa Fe Trail was opening (see Chapter 2), William Henry Ashley, a general in the Missouri state militia, placed an

Fur trappers, such as this one in a Frederic Remington illustration, were the first Europeans to venture into the western American areas.

advertisement in a St. Louis newspaper. It was a call for "Enterprising Young Men...to ascend the Missouri to its source, there to be employed for one, two, or three years."

Like Manuel Lisa ten years earlier, Ashley was going up the Missouri River in search of beaver. But the general was offering his recruits a short-term contract. Instead of working for Ashley, these mountain men were free agents. They could keep half of whatever furs they collected. Ashley would provide them with guns and powder and other necessities. In return, the trappers had to agree to help him build a fort and defend it as necessary.

Like Lisa, Ashley planned to build his fort and trading post where the Yellowstone and Missouri Rivers met, on the border between present-day North Dakota and Montana. From there, the trappers could spread out to search for beaver. But the plan failed. Long before Ashley's keelboats reached the Yellowstone River, warriors at the Arikara villages met the intruders with rifles and arrows. In the fierce battle that followed, 14 of Ashley's men were killed before the boats could retreat back down the river.

Ashley was forced to give up his plan for a fort far up the Missouri River. Instead, he established a temporary fort, Fort Kiowa, about 150 miles downriver from the Arikara villages. From Fort Kiowa, in what is now South Dakota, Ashley sent his men overland to look for good trapping areas. The men agreed to join Ashley the following summer at a rendezvous (meeting) to trade their furs for ammunition and other supplies. Thus began the central Rocky Mountain fur trade. And with the trapping would come more exploring and trailblazing.

While one company of Ashley's trappers headed northwest from Fort Kiowa toward the Yellowstone River, Jedediah Strong Smith led the other company straight

Mountain Men Rendezvous

Once a year the mountain men came down out of the mountains to a rendezvous, or trappers' get-together, where they sold their furs to traders, collected supplies to last another year, and caught up on the news of fellow trappers. Some mountain men worked independently. Others worked for English or American fur companies that operated trading posts in the western wilderness in the early 1800s. The rendezvous was like a fair—trappers went there not only to trade but to have fun. During the two or three week celebration, a thousand or more mountain men, traders, and Native Americans and their families might attend. When the rendezvous was over, the mountain men would decide when and where they would meet the following summer. They then spent the winter collecting beaver skins, returning the next June or July to the rendezvous to trade their winter's harvest of furs for traps, guns, ammunition, knives, tobacco, and other necessities.

Mountain men or fur trappers got together occasionally
to trade furs and tales around the campfire.

west, through the present Badlands National Park and Black Hills National Forest of southwestern South Dakota. With Smith were Thomas Fitzpatrick, who was second in command, William Sublette, James Clyman, and eight other men.

Jed Smith, a 24-year-old woodsman from New York State, had headed west to become an explorer after reading an account of the Lewis and Clark Expedition. But he soon learned that the life of a mountain man was not only exciting—but also dangerous. Smith was one of those who were sent ashore during the battle with the Arikara a few months before. That time, he barely escaped with his life as he tossed rifle and equipment into the water and swam frantically downstream to catch the retreating keelboat.

Then, in the Black Hills, Smith was attacked by an enraged grizzly bear. The grizzly seized Smith's whole head in its jaws. Before others in Smith's company came to the rescue, the grizzly tore off Smith's scalp and one of his ears. Jim Clyman used needle and thread to stitch up most of the wounds, and Smith insisted he also try somehow to sew the ear back on. Clyman later reported how he stuck the needle "through and through and over and over," laying the

People venturing into the mountains of the West were careful not to confront or enrage a grizzly bear.

lacerated parts together "as nice as I could." Soon after, Smith was able to mount his horse and ride to a camp a mile away, where the men pitched the only tent they had. Here, according to Clyman, they tried to make Smith "as comfortable as circumstances would permit." After ten days, the injured man was recovered enough for the company to continue working its way west through the mountains of present northern Wyoming, exploring and trapping.

By November, Jed Smith and his company ended up in the valley of the Wind River, in present western Wyoming. At a Crow village, the trappers were told of the many beaver in the valley of the Green River, called Seedskeedee by the Indians. Smith hoped to go there that winter. But the weather turned severe, so instead the company spent the winter in the skin lodges (tepees made of buffalo hides) at the Crow village.

The next February, Smith's party tried to cross the mountains to get to the Seedskeedee valley. But they failed. They returned to the Crow villages to ask for help. Spreading a deerskin on the ground for a map, Smith used piles of sand for mountain peaks as he tried to get directions for getting over the Wind River range.

On the makeshift "map" the Crows showed the trappers an easy route across the mountains farther down the valley. The mountain pass turned out to be the same one that Robert Stuart had found, with the help of Native Americans, a dozen years earlier while traveling from west to east. Smith and the others had never learned about Stuart's discovery because fur trader John Jacob Astor had kept it secret. Astor did not believe in sharing information about his trading business with his competition—including other American traders and trappers.

Jed Smith and his company crossed the pass in a blizzard, with freezing winds and heavy snowfall. But the next day Smith saw that water in a stream was flowing west, and he knew that he had crossed the Continental Divide. This is the backbone of the mountains that runs the entire length of the Rockies. Streams east of the Divide flow east, toward the Mississippi River; streams west of the Divide flow west, toward the Pacific Ocean.

Smith's company easily descended from South Pass to the Seedskeedee valley to trap for beaver. When summer came, they joined fellow trappers at Ashley's rendezvous. The big news Jed Smith had to share was his crossing of South Pass. From then on, this wide gap in the mountains became the main way for the mountain men to cross the central Rockies.

By the late 1840s, South Pass had become the accepted gateway to the West. The many paths discovered by Jedediah Smith and the other mountain men became the routes that emigrants followed to the Oregon Country and California.

⊕

TWO

Caravans West:
The Santa Fe
and Gila Trails

During the time the Spanish ruled what is now the southwestern United States—from about 1600 to the early 1800s—they tried to keep all foreigners out. Santa Fe, capital and only town of the Spanish province of Nuevo Mexico (New Mexico), remained isolated from the outside world. That frustrated the French traders of the Mississippi River valley. Almost from the time that France claimed the region in 1682, the French wanted to trade with their Spanish neighbors to the west. They were especially eager to sell their goods to merchants in Santa Fe.

Unfortunately for the French, only Spanish traders were allowed in Santa Fe. These traders hauled their goods from Mexico City over the *camino real*, or "king's road," by caravan—a train of pack mules and wagons. With no competition, the Spanish traders could charge the people in Santa Fe as much as they wished for the fine cloth, jewelry, guns, and other manufactured goods they brought north.

Despite the law forbidding foreigners on Spanish territory, a few French traders managed to sneak into Santa Fe in the late 1700s and early 1800s. Most sold their goods quickly for a profit and left before they could be arrested. Others, not so lucky, ended up in Spanish jails there.

In 1806, at the same time Lewis and Clark were returning from their expedition to the northwest part of the Louisiana Territory, army lieutenant Zebulon Montgomery Pike was sent by Louisiana's governor to explore the southwest part of the new territory. Like Lewis and Clark, Pike started from St. Louis, where the Missouri and Mississippi Rivers meet. In the summer of 1806, Pike and 15 enlisted men poled up the Missouri—that is, pushed their keelboat upstream by using long poles. In a short time they left the Missouri River and poled up the Osage River, through what is now the state of Kansas.

Zebulon Pike sighted the mountain named after him in 1806. He was killed during the War of 1812 while attacking York (now Toronto).

Continuing west to present-day Colorado, Pike saw, but did not climb, the mountain now known as Pikes Peak. Turning south, Pike and his men found themselves in the Sangre de Cristo Mountains on the border between the present states of Colorado and New Mexico. Winter

The snow dappled mountain in the background was named Pikes Peak in memory of Zebulon Pike's explorations in the area.

snowstorms struck and for three months the group battled the cold. Nine of the men froze their feet before they finally found their way out of the mountains—only to be arrested by a Spanish cavalry patrol.

By mistake, Pike had wandered into Nuevo Mexico (New Mexico), which was Spanish territory. The Spanish did not take kindly to foreign intruders, and the cavalry patrol took Pike to Santa Fe. He was well-treated and soon released, but only after he had a good look at Santa Fe. Pike had time to note how expensive imported goods were: $20 for a yard of fine cloth, $1 for a pound of iron, $4 for a pound of tobacco. On the other hand, he saw that local products such as flour, wine, and salt, were inexpensive. So were New Mexican sheep, beef cattle, and mules.

Pike published a report of his adventures in 1810. When American traders read it and learned about the high prices for imported goods in Santa Fe, they were as eager as the French to trade there. Right away, a few North Americans set off for Santa Fe. But like the French traders before them, the North Americans were arrested and put in jail.

Then, in the fall of 1821, soon after Missouri became a state, Captain William Becknell had an amazing bit of good luck. With four companions, Becknell left Franklin, a new and bustling town along the Missouri River in the center of the state, to hunt, trap, and possibly to capture wild horses in what is now Colorado. Becknell took along a few pack animals loaded with trade items, in case he met Comanches who wanted to barter. Instead of Indians, Becknell met some friendly soldiers who appeared to be Spanish. Although Becknell and the others spoke no Spanish, they got the impression from the soldiers that they would now be safe in Santa Fe. So the traders accompanied the soldiers to the provincial capital. There they met a French resident who became their interpreter. With his help at translating, Becknell and the others learned that two months earlier there had been a revolution. The people of Mexico had thrown out the Spanish rulers and taken control of their country including the province of Nuevo Mexico. The Mexicans were now ready and willing to trade with the people from Missouri. Becknell displayed the few items he had meant to trade with the Indians. Mexicans gladly bought everything he had, paying in silver and offering amounts far higher than the goods originally cost.

The next spring William Becknell again went to Santa Fe to trade. This time he loaded merchandise into three wagons, which meant he could haul more without the nuisance of unloading the pack mules each night when he made camp. But taking wagons meant Becknell had to find a new route.

On his first trip west, Becknell had cut across what is now the state of Kansas until he came to the great bend of the Arkansas River. He had followed the river west into present-day Colorado. He had then crossed into New Mexico over Raton Pass in the Rocky Mountains. Urging the pack animals over the narrow, twisting mountain pass had been difficult enough. Becknell knew he could never do it with wagons.

On this second trip, Becknell blazed a more direct, less mountainous, route to Santa Fe. As before, he stayed close to the Arkansas River until he neared the present town of Dodge City, Kansas. Then, instead of continuing west he left the Arkansas River to cross a flat, dry plain to the Cimarron River in what is now southwestern Kansas. From there, Becknell continued on to Santa Fe. The new short-cut, known as the "Cimarron Cutoff," saved 100 miles and avoided the treacherous Raton Pass. When the North

American trader reached Santa Fe, he once again quickly sold his goods for a handsome profit.

Having proved that wagons could safely make the 800-mile trip, Becknell went back to Santa Fe the next year. And other traders rounded up teams of oxen or mules and loaded wagons with supplies to follow his lead. A year later, still more Missouri merchants headed west on the trail to Santa Fe. The departure point had now shifted to Arrow Rock, a few miles upstream from Franklin.

By 1827 steamboats were able to bring merchandise from St. Louis all the way up the Missouri River to Independence, just east of today's Kansas City, Missouri, on the Missouri-Kansas border. At the wharves of Independence, merchants could transfer their boat cargo onto wagons or pack animals to begin the journey to Santa Fe.

Meanwhile, the U.S. Congress had voted to improve the entire Santa Fe Trail, even though much of the trail was on Mexican land. Federal commissioners had met with Osage chiefs at Council Grove, a wooded area about 150 miles west of Independence, to offer cash and goods for the right to pass through Osage land. And government surveyors had placed mounds of dirt and rocks to mark the route.

Unfortunately, wind and rain soon demolished the surveyors' dirt and rock markers, which most west-bound caravans chose to ignore, anyway. Concerned about saving time,

This engraving of 1840 shows a wagon train approaching the thriving town of Santa Fe.

the caravan leaders preferred a shortcut that shaved 30 miles off their journey and brought them to Santa Fe a day or two sooner. The most useful markers for the trail were the deep ruts made by wagon wheels after the especially heavy rains of 1834. In the next dry season, these ruts hardened to become permanent trail markers.

In the early years of the Santa Fe Trail one or two wagons might head west alone with only the trader and a few helpers—his sons or local boys looking for adventure. But Becknell persuaded the merchants it would be safer for several groups to travel together. Soon after, groups might set off separately but they would meet in Council Grove to elect a captain and officers for the caravan. Like a military officer, the captain then took charge. He assigned jobs, and decided which route to follow and where to camp at night.

With large caravans, the wagons were often run four abreast to help cut down on the dust. If trouble threatened, the wagons were kept in their columns and the drivers tightened their ranks. The trail cut through Native American territory, and there was always the danger of an attack by the Arapahoe, the Comanche, or others who had not made treaties with the United States and who resented newcomers invading their hunting lands and killing their buffalo.

By now, Independence—the starting-off point for the trail—had become the busiest city west of St. Louis. In the spring, traders, trappers, bullwhackers (drivers of oxen teams), and muleskinners (drivers of mule teams) crowded the main square as they prepared for their journey west. Heavy wagons, pulled by a dozen mules or six yoke of oxen, lumbered past, piled high with crates and boxes. A caravan's cargo might include mirrors, ladies' dress patterns from eastern magazines, silk, gingham, calico, and

The Conestoga Wagon

As merchants sent more freight to Santa Fe, they used larger and larger wagons. A favorite was the canvas-covered Conestoga wagon from Pennsylvania, with its tall wheels and iron tires. Wagons were drawn by a dozen mules, walking single file, or by a dozen oxen, two to a yoke. The mule driver sat on a high wagon seat behind the animals. For wagons drawn by oxen, the driver walked beside the animals. As he cracked his bullwhip over their backs, the sound was like a rifle shot.

The Conestoga wagon was the favorite means of transportation for most western travelers.

velvet, needles, knives, metal tools, books, and work shoes. Herded behind the wagons were spare animals, to replace any that were lost or stolen along the way.

The troubles that travelers faced on the trail were many—besides the possibility of an ambush there were rattlesnakes, violent winds, rainstorms, and thunderclaps that stampeded the livestock. Some streams were too flooded to cross, while in the desert there was so little water that animals might die of thirst. Despite the hazards, there was a sense of excitement and adventure when a wagon train left town to the sound of animal drivers snapping their long whips.

Oxen dying of thirst surely meant that this group of emigrants might need to continue on foot carrying what they could.

Besides trade items, merchants loaded on the wagons enough food staples for themselves, their helpers, and any visitors traveling west with the caravan. For each person they brought about 50 pounds of flour, 50 pounds of bacon, 10 pounds of coffee, and 20 pounds each of sugar and salt. For meat, they depended on buffalo hunts and shooting other game along the way.

Because the trail to Santa Fe was an important trade route, in the mid-1800s the U.S. government built several forts where traders could get supplies or repair

Abandoned in 1891, Fort Union (New Mexico) was one of the usual stops along the Santa Fe Trail.

The First Women on the Santa Fe Trail

Few women traveled on the Santa Fe Trail in the early years, although on his 1831 trip to Santa Fe, Josiah Gregg did meet "two respectable French ladies" and "a Spanish family." In 1846, 17-year-old Susan Shelby Magoffin followed the trail west with her new husband, trader Samuel Magoffin. The Magoffins had been married only six months and the journey was like an extension of their honeymoon. They traveled in style, with a luxurious tent furnished with cabinets, a bed, stools, and a carpet. Besides the Magoffin's carriage, the caravan included a smaller wagon for Susan's maid, Jane, a crate of live chickens for dinners along the way, 14 wagonloads of trade goods, and some 200 oxen, mules, and saddle horses.

Susan Magoffin kept a diary of the journey, which she later published. In it she describes the novel sights and sounds of the teamsters as the journey began, with "the cracking of whips, lowing of cattle, braying of mules, whooping and hollowing of the men." But the young, well-bred Mrs. Magoffin does admit to finding it "disagreeable to hear so much swearing." She endured more serious problems, too—her tent blowing over

their wagons. Soldiers patrolled the route, often accompanying the caravans to the Mexican border which was then at the Arkansas River.

The long and dusty journey to Santa Fe and back took the greater part of a year. The merchants left Missouri in the spring after the snow melted. This assured them of buffalo grass and other forage (food) along the way for the livestock. At night, the drivers often formed a circle of the wagons to keep the livestock safely inside.

The wagons arrived in Santa Fe in June or July. In the

in a cloudburst, millions of mosquitoes, snakes encountered on daily walks, and the trail sometimes so muddy that the wagons crept along at only one mile in an hour.

Three weeks out of Independence, Susan reports that—like most other travelers on the trail—she scratched her name on the soft surface of Pawnee Rock, known as "the prairie register." She delighted in being able to "breathe free without the oppression and uneasiness felt in the gossiping circles of a settled home."

In her diary, Susan Magoffin tells of walking in prairie grass as high as her waist as she gathered the raspberries and gooseberries that grew "in abundance," and of learning to make soup with hump ribs ("one of the choice parts of the buffalo!"). In the heat of the desert she saw for the first time mirages, which the traders called "false ponds." And when the caravan halted on Sundays, Susan Magoffin listened to the teamsters "singing the hymns perhaps they were taught by a pious good mother."

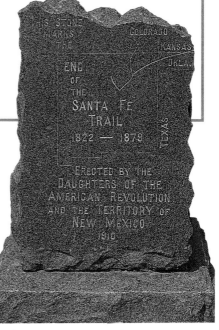

fall the merchants returned home with their profits along with buffalo and beaver skins and wool. Some bought sturdy Mexican mules and burros at a low price in Santa Fe, to sell at a profit to Missouri farmers.

Eventually, many merchants found that trade was more profitable in Mexican towns south of Santa Fe. Often in later years wagons

This marker indicates the end of the Santa Fe Trail in Santa Fe Plaza.

did not even stop at Santa Fe, but continued on down the *camino real* to El Paso del Norte, Chihuahua, or beyond. Some traders chose to sell their wagons and oxen in Mexico and buy a few pack mules for the journey back home. For the return trip, the traders usually had a much smaller load—any merchandise they bought plus coins, silver bars, and gold dust received in payment for their trade goods.

Unlike some other western trails, the Santa Fe Trail was mainly a trade route for merchants. Even so, trappers, gold-seekers, settlers, and soldiers also used the trail.

The Gila Trail

Thousands of years ago, Native American traders with shells and turquoise traveled along the valley of the Gila River in what is now southern Arizona. In the late 1600s and early 1700s when the Spanish controlled this area, the Jesuit priest Eusebio Francisco Kino made a journey west along the Gila River to the Colorado River. He was the first Spaniard to suggest that it was possible to travel overland between the Spanish colony of Nuevo Mexico, now New Mexico, and the Pacific shore. In 1774 another priest, Father Francisco Garcés, proved Kino right when he led Juan Bautista de Anza and a group of Spanish soldiers along the Gila until that river joined the Colorado River. From there Father Garcés and the others struck out across the sandy desert in the southeastern part of Upper California. Near what would later become Warner's Ranch they angled northwest to Mission San Gabriel in what is now greater Los Angeles.

For the next half century, few except Native Americans used the Gila Trail. Spanish traders and priests in Santa Fe preferred a more northerly route to Upper California by way of what are now the states of Utah and Nevada.

In 1824 Sylvestre Pattie and his son James Ohio Pattie became the first recorded North Americans to reach California by way of parts of the Gila Trail. The two men had come west to trap beaver on the Missouri River. Turned back at Council Bluffs on today's Iowa-Nebraska border for not having a trapping license, father and son joined a wagon train and went to Santa Fe instead. When James rescued a Mexican official's daughter who had been captured by Comanches, her grateful father allowed the Patties to trap in Mexican territory.

After trapping in the Rocky Mountains, the Patties tramped west along the Gila River valley to where the Gila and Colorado Rivers meet. But when they left the trail they found themselves lost in the California desert. They were close to dying of thirst when two Native Americans guided them to a Spanish mission in Lower California. There

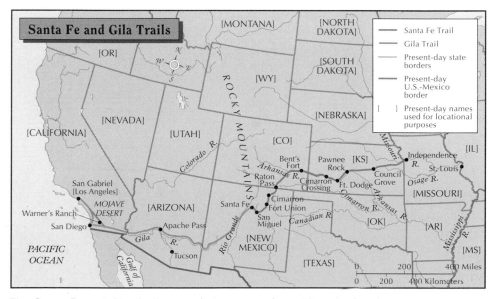

The Santa Fe and Gila Trails provided means of reaching the Pacific from Missouri in the late eighteenth and early nineteenth centuries.

soldiers arrested the two Patties and forced them to march north to San Diego, where they were put in jail.

Sylvestre Pattie died in the prison, but his son was eventually released and found his way back to Missouri. In 1831 James published a book about his adventures in the West. The Patties were not the first North Americans to travel overland to the California coast, however. Jedediah Smith, who came south and west to Los Angeles by way of the Great Salt Lake, beat them by three years!

When Congress declared war on Mexico in 1846, Colonel Stephen Watts Kearny had orders to occupy the territory from New Mexico to California. After taking Santa Fe without resistance, Kearny instructed one of his officers, Captain Philip St. George Cooke, to blaze a wagon trail from Santa Fe to San Diego. Under Cooke's command were 350 Mormon volunteers plus officers and wives, and

The Mormon Battalion was responsible for enlarging the Gila Trail south of Santa Fe so army supply wagons could use it during the Mexican War.

20 wagons. Staying close behind the surveyors and mappers, this Mormon batallion built the trail as they marched. With pickaxes and shovels they attacked dirt and stone as they hewed a road wide enough for army wagons—first, south from Santa Fe along the Rio Grande, and then angling southwest over mountains and arid tableland to Arizona's San Pedro River. But instead of going north to the Gila River, the men cut a trail straight west across 40 miles of desert to join the Gila at the town of Gila Bend. From there they followed the Gila west to the Colorado River, which they rafted across.

Half-starved and without water for three days and nights in the California desert, the soldiers of Cooke's batallion were exhausted by the time they reached Warner's Ranch. There, plenty of food and the warm mineral springs at the ranch revived them enough to go on to San Diego and complete the Gila Trail.

Later, a branch of the trail was established that led northwest from Warner's Ranch to Los Angeles. In the years that followed the wagon route built by the Mormon batallion was used by cattlemen, emigrants, surveyors, military commanders, mail carriers, and freighters hauling wagonloads of merchandise.

After gold was discovered in California, many prospectors took the Santa Fe Trail to Santa Fe, and then followed the Gila Trail to San Diego or Los Angeles. From both of these California towns travelers could board ships bound for San Francisco. Other gold seekers from the east pushed south from the Arkansas River to Texas, and headed west through El Paso before they picked up the Gila Trail and continued on to California.

THREE

The Old
Spanish Trail

In the late 1700s, when the Spanish still ruled the Southwest, they needed a trail that linked Santa Fe in Nuevo Mexico with Mission San Gabriel in Upper California. And so they created an overland route to the north and west that eventually could connect the two Spanish frontier outposts. American trappers and traders in the 1830s gave this route the name "Old Spanish Trail," although by the time the trail was completed, Mexico had broken away from Spain to become an independent country.

The route that became the Old Spanish Trail was long, crooked, and difficult to follow. It changed and grew as explorers and traders and trappers—Spanish or American—found an easier place to ford a river, took a different short cut, or located an easier mountain pass.

The first part of the trail, north from Santa Fe, was a traditional Indian trading route. The Native Americans had used it long before the Spanish arrived. In the 1760s, Spanish traders from Santa Fe followed the trail to the mountains and high plateaus of what are now southwestern Colorado and southeastern Utah, to trade with the Utes and other friendly Indians.

In 1776, the Spanish priests Fathers Escalante and Domínguez joined an expedition from Santa Fe that

followed the traditional traders' path north. Then Father
Escalante and the others left the trail to trudge farther
north through the Colorado Rockies to the White River,
just below the present Colorado-Wyoming border. From
here, the expedition went west. The Spanish explorers
came within a few miles of Great Salt Lake before turning
south and starting back to Santa Fe.

At the same time, another Spanish priest, Francisco
Garcés, began looking for a trail that would lead east
from Upper California to join the traders' trail from Santa
Fe. In 1775 Father Garcés had left his post at Mission of
San Xavier del Bac, near present day Tucson, Arizona, to
guide Spanish colonists partway to Upper California. He
led them along Arizona's Gila River valley as far west as
the Yuma villages on the Colorado River. Now, a year
later, Father Garcés decided to go north from the Yuma
villages to find out what was upriver.

With his Indian guides, Father Garcés traveled as far as
the Mojave villages just beyond the present town of
Needles, California, on the California-Arizona border. From
here, Mojave guides led the Spanish priest straight west
over early Indian bartering paths to Mission San Gabriel.

On a later exploration, Father Garcés left the Mojave
villages to go east to Arizona's Grand Canyon and beyond.
He still had hopes of opening a trail from the west to Santa
Fe, but he found the Arizona Hopis decidedly less friendly than the Mojaves. After they refused to provide the
priest with food or lodging, and even threatened to kill
him, Father Garcés gave up his trailblazing ideas.

Soon, the Yuma Indians also turned more hostile toward
the Spanish. For the time being, the idea of establishing a
trail between Mission San Gabriel and Santa Fe across
what is now southern Arizona was dropped. Instead, the

In this painting, Frederic Remington shows a wagon
train passing an adobe village (in the background)
occupied by Native Americans.

Spanish went back to establishing the more northerly trail
between the two frontier outposts, on the land of the
friendlier Ute Indians. It was this route that eventually
became the Old Spanish Trail.

From Santa Fe the trail was extended north and west
piece by piece as traders from Santa Fe visited Ute villages
to exchange horses for the Ute's buckskin, dried meat, furs,
and—occasionally—Indian slaves. Gradually, the Spanish
traders pushed the trail farther from Santa Fe and closer
to what became, in 1781, the town of Los Angeles, near
Mission San Gabriel. They found a way to cross the Colorado
River to near present-day Moab, Utah. From what is now
central Utah, they turned south and west. Much of the time
they followed a route Father Escalante had once taken.

By 1822, after Mexico won its freedom from Spain in
1821, trappers and traders from the United States began to
invade the southern Rockies to search for beaver. As they

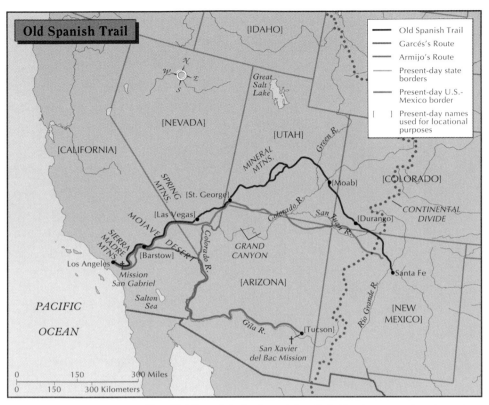

The Old Spanish Trail and Armijo's Route were developed as ways farther north to California.

crisscrossed the Old Spanish Trail, these mountain men made their own changes and additions. At different times, trappers developed parts of this early trail until at last the Old Spanish Trail reached all the way from Santa Fe to California. Jedediah Smith traveled over parts of the trail when he became the first recorded North American to make the trip overland to Upper California through the Southwest.

It was curiosity that brought mountain man Jed Smith to California. For besides being one of the most skilled of the American fur trappers, Smith was also a constant explorer. By the end of 1825 most trappers in the central Rockies knew about Great Salt Lake, although none of them knew what lay beyond the lake. In the summer of 1826, Jed Smith decided to find out. After the rendezvous at Cache Valley, Utah, Smith and his two partners split up. The partners went into the hills to hunt for beaver. Smith, with a party of 15 men, set out to discover what was south and west of Great Salt Lake. They made their way to the huge lake. From there, they continued south to the Sevier River in central Utah, then on to what is now Zion National Park.

Jedediah Smith's trek across the Mojave Desert in 1826 is depicted in this Frederic Remington painting.

Here, Smith and his men turned southwest and crossed the harsh desert until they came to the Colorado River. Some miles below what is now the southernmost tip of Nevada, the group came to the Mojave villages. There they met two Native Americans who offered to lead them through the California desert. The native guides followed an old trade route that led west to the Mission San Gabriel, the same route Father Garcés had taken to the mission in 1776.

By the time of Jedediah Smith's visit to Upper California in 1826, nearly 1,000 people had settled in Los Angeles, the town that had grown up near Mission San Gabriel. Although the local people were friendly, the Mexican governor took his time about meeting the North American trappers. So for about six weeks, Smith and the others relaxed and enjoyed fiestas (parties) and the mild climate and pleasant scenery of California.

On his return to the central Rockies, Smith chose to go north through California's inland valley at the edge of the Sierra Nevada. Smith had intended to lead his group east across the mountains at the American River, northeast of today's Sacramento. But when they started their crossing the first week in May, deep snow still covered the mountain passes. After he lost five horses and several men nearly froze to death trying to get across, Smith decided to

Disappearing Rivers

Often rivers that rise in the mountains and flow into the desert eventually lose themselves in the sand. These river sinks were the life-giving links that made travel across a wide, scorched desert possible for the early explorers and traders. The Mojave River flows down from the San Bernardino Mountains near Los Angeles to end in a desert sink more than 100 miles to the east. The Humboldt River, which begins in the mountains of northern Nevada, flows west across the desert of the Great Basin to form the Humboldt Sink less than 100 miles from California's Sierra Nevada Mountains.

An aerial view of the Humboldt Sink shows the lack of vegetation in this desolate area.

go farther south. There he settled most of his men in a camp along the Stanislaus River to wait for a thaw. Then with two companions and a few horses, Jed Smith made one more try at getting across the Sierras.

This time he made it, crossing at what is now Ebbet's Pass, about 40 miles south of Lake Tahoe. Now, the three faced a threat of a different sort. Before them, the nearly treeless and waterless Great Basin stretched for hundreds of miles. Long before the men reached Utah's Wasatch

Bristlecone pines furnish the only greenery in this recent photo of the Great Basin in Nevada.

Mountains to the east, they ran out of both food and water, and several of their horses died in the desert heat. When one of the three men, Robert Evans, fell and could go no farther, the others had no choice but to leave him stretched out under the shade of a small cedar tree. Then they pressed on, in hopes of finding water. By luck, a few miles farther on they did find water. They hurried back to revive Evans, then the three trudged on until they reached the south shore of Great Salt Lake. Jedediah Smith had managed to cross the continent's highest mountains and its widest desert to return to the spot from which he had departed the year before.

And he had done it without instruments, without guides after leaving Mission San Gabriel, and without trails to follow.

In a few months, Jed Smith was back on the same trail to Upper California that he had taken before. On leaving this time, however, Smith did not go across the California Sierra Nevadas. Instead, he went north to explore what is now Oregon. On his return to the central Rockies he circled

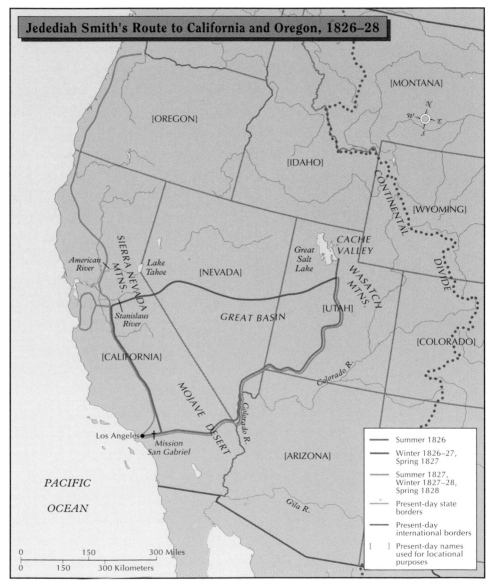

Over three years Jedediah Smith recorded trails from Utah to California and as far north as present-day Oregon.

across present-day northeast Washington and northern Idaho, and even ducked briefly over today's international border into Canada.

By the time Smith was back from his second visit to Upper California, news of his first visit had reached traders in Santa Fe. And already the Spanish trader Antonio Armijo was planning to take a packtrain of goods over Smith's trail to trade with the Californians.

Armijo began his journey from Santa Fe to Los Angeles in 1829. Instead of swinging northwest through the present states of Colorado and Utah, as earlier traders from Santa Fe had done, Armijo traveled a straighter route (see map on page 39), staying close to what are now the northern borders of New Mexico and Arizona. He crossed "Four Corners," where the corners of the states of Colorado, Utah, Arizona, and New Mexico now meet. With his shortcut, Armijo slashed hundreds of miles from the previous route.

Near what is now St. George, in the southeastern corner of Utah, Armijo crossed over the trail Jed Smith had blazed a few years earlier. For a few miles Armijo followed Smith's trail, He did not go all the way to the Mojave villages before turning west, as Jed Smith (and Father Garcés before him) had done. Instead, Armijo took another shortcut, and angled southwest from present-day Las Vegas, Nevada. In the Nevada desert, Armijo ran out of food. Before they finally reached Los Angeles, he and his men were forced to kill a horse or a mule every few days to keep from starving.

Antonio Armijo's journey from Santa Fe to Los Angeles took three months. From Santa Fe, which was in sheep country, he had brought woolen fabric and wool blankets. These he traded in Upper California for silk and other goods the Californians had imported from China, and also for horses and mules that had been raised on California ranches. Back in Santa Fe, these California animals caused a flurry of excitement, because they were much larger and stronger than mules and burros from other parts of Mexico.

Once Armijo had opened the Old Spanish Trail to trade, caravans from Santa Fe regularly headed for Los Angeles each fall and spring. Because of the desert heat, summer travel was never safe. And few attempted the trail in the winter, although William Wolfskill, the first North American to travel the entire length of the Old Spanish Trail, was willing to try.

In the late fall of 1830 Wolfskill decided to go to the south-central area of Upper California to trap beaver. Since heavy snow made crossing the Sierra Nevada Mountains impossible, Wolfskill and his party went west over the Spanish Trail instead. They almost did not make it. Often they had to break a path through drifts two or three feet deep. They ran out of provisions, and like Armijo ended up eating their horses and mules. But three months later, in January of 1831, the Wolfskill party finally made it to Los Angeles.

FOUR

The Emigrant
Road West

By the 1830s, people in the eastern part of the United States knew a great deal about the once-unknown land beyond the Mississippi River. The report of Meriwether Lewis and William Clark had been published, as had the diary of Sergeant Gass, who was with the expedition. Easterners had read the personal narratives of several mountain men and Indian fighters, and dozens of romantic books and newspaper articles written about them. Museums showed specimens of western animals and plants, and the drawings of scientific illustrators such as Titian Ramsey Peale—who went with a military expedition by steamboat up the Missouri River in 1819.

Art galleries also displayed the works of artist George Catlin, who had lived among the Blackfeet for a season and did paintings of Indian dances, feasts, and ceremonies as well as portraits of their chief and other Indian dignitaries. By the 1830s even European artists and writers had started to visit the American West and had begun to record their impressions in words and pictures.

Besides reading about the West and looking at paintings and sketches, some people east of the frontier had actually sailed around the tip of South America to settle in the Oregon Country. As early as 1818, a Boston teacher named

"Competition among the Mandans" by George Catlin pictured these western North Dakota Indians in an archery contest.

Hall Jackson Kelley tried to persuade congressmen to vote for United States occupation of the entire Pacific Northwest. Instead, Congress merely agreed that year to share control of the Oregon Country with England. Undaunted, Kelley started his own "American Society for Encouraging the Settlement of Oregon," and went to work on plans for establishing an American colony on the Columbia River.

In 1830, mountain man Jedediah Smith and his two partners at that time, David Jackson and William Sublette, wrote a long letter to the United States secretary of war praising the wonders of the West. Smith reported that he had found San Francisco most delightful and pleasant, with fertile farmland across the bay. He and his partners listed the good qualities of the Oregon Country, noting the number of cattle and horses they had seen, and the fields of corn and grain. The three mountain men seemed to encourage American settlement of the West, for in their letter they described how easy it would be for not only wagons to cross the Rocky Mountains by way of the South Pass, but also herds of cattle and milk cows!

A year after the Smith-Jackson-Sublette letter, the enthusiastic businessman Hall Jackson Kelley published his 28-page *Manual of the Oregon Expedition—A General Circular to all Persons of Good Character, who wish to Emigrate to the Oregon Territory.* Although Kelley had never been to the Oregon Country, he, too, described its wonders to potential settlers.

Not long after, the army gave Captain Benjamin Bonneville leave from his military duties to go west. Supposedly, Bonneville was to learn about the various Indian groups, the climate, the geography, and other features of the West. Some historians believe the army officer's real assignment was to find out if it was possible for Americans to settle in the Far West. Whatever the true reason for his trip west, Bonneville became a fur trapper and trader—and also did considerable exploring. In May of 1832 Bonneville brought a caravan of wagons over the South Pass—the first wagons to cross the Continental Divide.

A

GENERAL CIRCULAR

TO ALL

PERSONS OF GOOD CHARACTER,

WHO WISH TO EMIGRATE

TO THE

OREGON TERRITORY,

EMBRACING SOME ACCOUNT OF THE CHARACTER AND
ADVANTAGES OF THE COUNTRY; THE RIGHT
AND THE MEANS AND OPERATIONS BY
WHICH IT IS TO BE SETTLED;—

AND

ALL NECESSARY DIRECTIONS FOR BECOMING

AN EMIGRANT.

Hall J. Kelley, General Agent.

BY ORDER OF THE AMERICAN SOCIETY FOR ENCOURAGING

the SETTLEMENT of the OREGON TERRITORY.

INSTITUTED IN BOSTON, A.D. 1829.

CHARLESTOWN:

PRINTED BY WILLIAM W. WHEILDON.
R. P. & C. WILLIAMS—BOSTON.
1831.

The cover of Hall Jackson Kelley's circular encouraging people to emigrate to the Oregon Country.

At the 1833 rendezvous, Bonneville hired veteran mountain man Joseph Reddeford Walker to find a trail to Upper California, which was still part of Mexico. The trail that Walker blazed was to become the gateway for California-bound settlers. Joe Walker left Great Salt Lake in July of 1833 with a party of 60 trappers. He started across the Great Basin—the wide stretch of desert that lies between Utah's Wasatch Mountains and the Sierra Nevada Mountains of California. Walker's route was many miles north of the part of the Great Basin that Jed Smith had crossed in 1826. Walker went west along the Humboldt River, which had been discovered only a few years before by the Canadian explorer and trapper Peter Skene Ogden.

The Walker party continued following the Humboldt south and west until the river turned into the marshy Humboldt Sink east of the California Sierra Nevada Mountains. The trappers crossed the Sierra Nevadas in late October, probably near the present Tioga Pass. Already the snow was deep. Men and horses floundered through the high drifts, making almost no progress. Discouraged, Walker's men nearly gave up and went back to the Great Basin.

Instead, however, they stumbled on. Eventually they found themselves in what is now Yosemite National Park. Joseph Walker and his trappers were probably the first non-Native Americans to see Yosemite's natural

Giant redwoods, such as these in Sequoia National Park, were found by early pioneers in many California locales.

wonders. They were astounded to find giant redwood trees that measured "sixteen to eighteen fathoms [about 100 feet] round the trunk."

Walker led his group across what is now the state of California to the Pacific Coast. Mexican authorities in Monterey received them kindly, permitting them to stay there and rest from their exhausting journey.

On his return trip, Walker's group consisted of 52 men, 300 horses, about 400 cattle, and many dogs. Walker first led them south along the San Joaquin River. At the very southern tip of the Sierra Nevada Mountains, they turned east. Walker made the gradual climb and an easy crossing through a natural gap in the mountains near what is now the central California town of Bakersfield. The pass later came to be called Walker's Pass, and became the gateway to the southern Sierras for California-bound settlers.

Beyond the pass, Walker and his men headed north toward the Humboldt Sink. Over the grueling desert crossing, they suffered greatly from thirst. Walker later described that when an animal died the men "would immediately catch the blood and greedily drink it down." By the time that part of the journey was over, Walker had lost 64 horses, 10 cows, and 15 dogs—but no men.

About the time Joseph Walker was exploring California, in 1833, a New York newspaper, the *Christian Advocate*, published a story about four Nez Perce who had traveled all the way to St. Louis from the Pacific Northwest to ask their friend William Clark a question. They were Native Americans who had met Clark—now superintendent of the Bureau of Indian Affairs—on his expedition 30 years before. Was it true that the white men had a book, the Indians asked, a book that would tell them the right way to worship the Great Spirit?

Members of Protestant churches who read the newspaper account realized that the book the Nez Perce wondered about was the Bible. Immediately various Protestant leaders put out a call for missionaries to go west to Oregon Country to teach the Native Americans about Christianity.

One eager volunteer was Jason Lee, a Methodist from Vermont, who was teaching church school in Quebec. To raise money for his mission, Lee gave speeches at churches and camp meetings throughout the East. By 1834 Lee had enough funds for the journey, so he hired Nathaniel Wyeth of Boston as a guide and made plans to go west and become a missionary to the Native Americans.

At one time Wyeth had worked with Hall Johnson Kelley, who back in 1831 proposed starting a colony in the Oregon Country. At that time Wyeth had even signed up to guide Kelley's colonists west. But after Kelley kept putting off the departure date, the exasperated Wyeth gave up and became a fur trader. By the time he met Jason Lee, Wyeth had already made one trip west in an unsuccessful attempt to get his trading business started.

In the spring of 1834 Nathaniel Wyeth was anxious to make a second try at fur trading. This time he took along Jason Lee. On April 28 he set out from Independence, Missouri, with trading goods to sell to the trappers at the Green River rendezvous. Besides Wyeth and Lee were Lee's nephew Daniel, the men working for Wyeth, and two scientists—Dr. Nuttall, a botanist (plant expert) who wanted to collect western plants for the Harvard Botanical Gardens, and Dr. Townsend, an ornithologist (bird expert).

From Independence the expedition followed the standard trappers' route—heading northwest along the valley of the Little Blue River to the Platte River near the present Nebraska towns of Kearney and Hastings. After

Independence Rock, shown in this contemporary engraving,
was a milestone on the western trail.

mule-drawn supply wagons passed Wyeth's camp one
night, a worried Wyeth spurred his own teams on. He was
not about to let another trader beat him to the Green River
rendezvous!

At the junction of the North Platte and Laramie Rivers
in what is now Wyoming, Wyeth saw something that dis-
tressed him greatly. Men who worked for the trapper and
trader William Sublette were building a fort. A few days
later, Wyeth's supply train reached Independence Rock, a
large, rounded mass of granite along the trappers' road
given its name by mountain men who celebrated the
Fourth of July—Independence Day—there in 1830. Several
mountain men had already scratched their names on the
rock, but one name and date Wyeth saw on the rock gave
him a shock. It was Sublette's, and he had been there only
three days before!

Knowing he had no time to lose, Wyeth tore through the valley of the Sweetwater River and rushed across South Pass to the trappers' meeting on the Green River. But despite his record-breaking journey from Independence—51 days—Wyeth was dismayed to find that William Sublette had beaten him there. So Sublette, and not he, would get the trappers' furs.

A dejected Wyeth, stuck with goods he could not trade, left soon after and at the junction of the Portneuf and Snake Rivers in present-day Idaho started construction of his own trading post. He called it Fort Hall. Leaving several of his company to finish the job and start trade with friendly Bannock and Snake Indians, Wyeth continued west. At Fort Vancouver in today's western Oregon he delivered Jason and Daniel Lee.

Soon after his arrival in the Oregon Country, Jason Lee established a farm and a sawmill in the valley of the Willamette River. This became the start of the first American settlement in Oregon Country. And its founder was not the would-be colonist Hall Jackson Kelley, but the missionary-turned-businessman Jason Lee.

A year after Jason Lee went west, two other eastern missionaries joined a party of westbound mountain men. They were Dr. Marcus Whitman, a Presbyterian, and Samuel Parker, a Congregationalist. The two missionaries attended a rendezvous at Green River where Dr. Whitman met mountain man Jim Bridger and removed a three-inch-long arrowhead from his back. The arrowhead

Noted mountain man Jim Bridger was probably the first white man to visit the Great Salt Lake.

had been lodged there since Bridger had fought with some Indians three years before.

Marcus Whitman put his few months in the wilderness to good use. He learned the tricks of wilderness survival and also realized it was possible for a family to travel by wagon over the passes of the Rocky Mountains. While Parker went on west to the Oregon Country, Marcus Whitman returned to New York.

The next year Whitman came back west with his new bride, Narcissa, and another missionary couple, Henry and Eliza Spalding. The four traveled from New York to Council Bluffs on the Missouri River, crossed the river by ferry, then loaded their goods on a heavy farm wagon and themselves into a lighter two-horse vehicle. Along the north side of Nebraska's Platte River, about 80 miles west of Council Bluffs, the missionaries caught up with the wagon train of mountain man Thomas Fitzpatrick, who was heading for the 1836 rendezvous at Green River with trade goods. His supplies had come up the Missouri River by steamboat to Council Bluffs. There he had loaded them onto wagons and pack mules.

Fitzpatrick was in a hurry to reach the rendezvous and begin trading. The missionaries, who had trouble keeping up, generally found themselves "eating the dust" at the rear. Fitzpatrick found the wagons—those of the missionaries as well as his own—a nuisance. To haul wagons and supplies over the Platte when they reached the mouth of the Laramie River in present-day Wyoming, his men lashed together two hollowed-out logs as a makeshift ferry.

Even more of a problem than hazardous river crossings was pulling the wagons over steep slopes and through thick woodlands. On a steep slope the men had to dig a rut to keep the wagons' wheels from skidding off. And to make a wagon trail through the woods they had to cut down trees. At Fort Laramie, Fitzpatrick was relieved to unload his goods onto pack mules and leave his wagons behind. Although Marcus Whitman agreed to give up the heavy farm wagon and repack the baggage onto pack mules, he insisted on keeping the smaller horse-drawn wagon.

A few days later, the Fitzpatrick caravan crossed South Pass. It had been 12 years since the snowy day in early spring of 1824 when Fitzpatrick, Jedediah Smith, William Sublette, and a small band of trappers first found the pass. In her diary Eliza Spalding noted the 1836 crossing over the ridge of land of the divide, which separated waters that flow into the Mississippi from those that flow into the Pacific. Once across South Pass, all those in the party considered themselves officially in the Oregon Country.

As soon as Fitzpatrick reached the rendezvous at Green River, he turned the missionaries and their wagon over to

Terrain such as this steep ravine was often encountered by wagon trains hauling emigrants to the west.

trappers working for the British Hudson's Bay Company. These men led the Whitmans and the Spaldings on west. At the Bear River near Soda Springs in what is now Idaho, the front axle on Whitman's small, four-wheeled wagon broke. He built a makeshift cart on the two rear wheels. Beyond Fort Boise, a Hudson's Bay Company trading post near present-day Idaho's western border, the narrow trails forced Whitman to abandon even his two-wheeled cart. He had to continue on with pack animals only.

The two couples chose different sites for their missions. The Spaldings started their mission and school among the Nez Perce at Lapwai, in Idaho's Clearwater River valley. Marcus and Narcissa Whitman chose the land of the Cayuse, to the north and west. The site was in what is now the southeast corner of Washington, near Fort Walla Walla, another Hudson's Bay Company trading post. Eventually their mission would become a favorite stopover for Oregon-bound emigrants who needed rest, supplies, and medical help.

As the number of emigrants increased, numerous wagons loaded to the hilt with supplies and furniture were common sights on the trail.

By the 1840s, people living east of the frontier were growing ever more familiar with life west of the Mississippi and Missouri Rivers. From time to time Marcus Whitman, Jason Lee, and other settlers returned east by horseback to give firsthand accounts of life in the West and to stir up interest in the Oregon Country. They managed to persuade many easterners to move west, especially after Nathaniel Wyeth had proved that the "trappers' route" across the mountains was safe to follow. Many books about the West also influenced Americans to emigrate west.

The emigrants who moved to the Oregon Country or Upper California in the late 1830s and early 1840s had many reasons. Crop prices dropped sharply after the depression of 1837, leaving many farmers and shop owners nearly destitute. Reports of the rich soil of Oregon lured poor dirt farmers from Missouri. Some people wanted to go west to get away from dirty, crowded cities, or from the diseases of the damp and cold Missouri and Mississippi valleys. Many simply saw the hope of a better life in the West.

The first organized company of emigrants to venture into the Far West were members of the Western Emigration Society. They had formed the society in Missouri in the winter of 1840, after they heard a fur trapper named Antoine Robidoux describe the wonders of California. The old trapper told of fields of grass and sweet clover in California, bands of horses and cows that ran wild, grapes in abundance, orchards of orange and olive trees—and especially, the mild climate.

At first, 500 people had signed up with the society to emigrate west. Most were from Missouri, but some were from as far away as Illinois and Kentucky. But as the company prepared to depart, in the spring of 1841, the number of emigrants had dropped to under 60 men,

No Shortage of Guides

Fortunately for most people who went to the Oregon Country or California in the early 1840s there was no shortage of guides. For by that time, the price of fur had fallen because there was little demand for it. The fashion-conscious English dandies and trendsetters had discarded their beaver hats for a newer fad: top hats made of silk.

Even if fur prices had not fallen, there were few beaver left to hunt, since by then the West had been almost completely "trapped out." Forced to find other work, many trappers and traders became wagon-train scouts for the emigrants who were starting to head west.

Mountain men made excellent guides. In their search for beaver they had gotten to know the Far West very well. They had mapped—in their heads, if not on paper—the entire Rockies including routes to California and the Oregon Country. With this knowledge, they were able to guide others.

women, and children. Although former schoolteacher and farmer John Bidwell had organized the group, wealthy John Bartleson refused to go unless he was elected their leader—and so he was.

On May 12, 1841, the Bidwell-Bartleson company gathered at Sapling Grove, Kansas, on the Santa Fe Trail, 20 miles west of Independence, the last settlement on the western frontier. There were 13 covered wagons drawn by mules, horses, or oxen. The wagons were crammed with the supplies the emigrants expected to need on the long journey. Among the barrels of bacon, sugar, and other foods was less than a barrel of flour per person—not enough, as it turned out.

The members of the Bidwell-Bartleson company were badly organized, with no clear idea of which way to go. Some opted for continuing on the Santa Fe Trail to California. Others wanted to find the trappers' road to the Rocky Mountains, and then head to California from there.

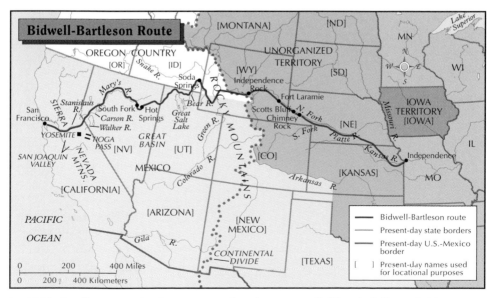

In 1841, the first organized company of emigrants to California followed this route.

No one seemed to have a reliable map. Fortunately, as company members argued, the caravan of Captain Thomas Fitzpatrick passed by. This time the veteran mountain man and trader was guiding Father Pierre Jean DeSmet and two of his fellow Catholic missionaries to northwestern Idaho. The Bidwell-Bartleson group hired Fitzpatrick to be their guide, too.

As the captain in charge, Fitzpatrick decided when and where to stop each night, and when to rise and leave the next morning. Usually the group camped on a wooded riverbank so there would be plenty of drinking water and wood for cooking. At night the wagons were parked to form a circle or a square to enclose the pack animals and keep them from straying.

After nearly two weeks on the trail, another wagon caught up with Fitzpatrick's group. The five men with the wagon asked if they, too, could join the caravan and Fitzpatrick agreed. One of the young newcomers was 31-year-old Joseph B. Chiles, a Kentuckian who had been a Missouri farmer.

Thomas Fitzpatrick followed the usual trappers' route, angling northwest to the south bank of the Platte River, and then following the Platte west to the North Platte. The emigrants passed Chimney Rock and Scott's Bluff, unusual

Scott's Bluff, Nebraska, must have been an imposing sight to western travelers. Here the landmark is shown in a recent photo with some wagons of the time.

rock formations in what is now western Nebraska. In later years these would become well-known landmarks for west-bound emigrants. On June 22, the company reached Fort Laramie, the outpost that American fur trader William Sublette and his partner Robert Campbell had built seven years earlier. A few miles beyond, the wagons had to ford the flood-swollen North Platte River.

The next important landmark for the emigrants was Independence Rock, where the Sweetwater River meets the North Platte. After time-out for the travelers to scratch their names on the rock, the wagons rumbled along the Sweetwater to South Pass. The emigrants had no problems getting their animals up the easy grade of the wide mountain pass, and along the way there was plenty of grass and water. After they crossed the pass they came to a spring, and were surprised and pleased to see that the water was now flowing west, toward the Pacific Ocean.

Beyond South Pass, the caravan came to Green River, site of mountain men rendezvous in the 1820s and 1830s.

A westward bound emigrant family makes evening camp on the trail.

Then it continued to the bubbling waters of Soda Springs. Here, some of the emigrants left Fitzpatrick's caravan. Although half of the Bidwell-Bartleson company had decided to go on to the Oregon Country, about 30 members of the group stuck to their original plan and headed south toward California. They included Bartleson, Bidwell, Chiles, and one family—Benjamin and Nancy Kelsey and their year-old baby daughter Ann.

Without a map and with no guide, the group heading for California searched for what seemed like the best route. As they crossed the desert west of Great Salt Lake, water holes grew farther and farther apart and often the water was rather salty. There was almost no grass for the half-starved animals. By the time the emigrants finally reached the Sierra Nevada Mountains of California, they had abandoned their wagons and were so low on food that they were forced to kill and eat the remaining pack animals. Although hopelessly lost much of the time and nearly starving, everyone survived—including Nancy Kelsey, walking barefoot as she carried her baby daughter. Just when it seemed they would never reach their destination, the lost emigrants stumbled into California's San Joaquin Valley.

Despite their near disaster, this part of the Bidwell-Bartleson company had made it to California. And their fellow emigrants had made it to the Willamette Valley, even though they had to abandon their wagons after Fort Hall. The two sections of the original Bidwell-Bartleson company had made it all the way to the Far West from Independence, Missouri. In the next five or six years, thousands more would follow their lead along the trappers' road, which as more emigrants began to go west would be called the Emigrant Road.

FIVE

The Oregon Trail

In 1842, a year after the two branches of the Bidwell-Bartleson company had managed—just barely—to make it from Missouri all the way to the Willamette Valley and to California, another company of 110 emigrants waited at the banks of the Missouri River. With 18 wagons and large herds of cattle, they hoped to settle in the Willamette Valley in the Oregon Country.

Leader of this second organized emigration company was Dr. Elijah White. Dr. White had been a missionary with Jason Lee, and afterward had become an Indian agent for the Oregon Country. His company left Independence on May 16, when they were sure prairie grasses would be high enough for livestock to feed on along the way. A late spring departure also meant they would cross the western mountains before winter snows closed all the passes.

By this time west-bound emigrants, while not sure of everything that lay ahead, had learned much about traveling west. They knew there were three forts along the way—Fort Laramie, Fort Hall, and Fort Boise—where they could rest and repair their wagons. The emigrants also knew how important it was to elect an experienced person as leader, and to have a set of rules everyone in the company had to follow.

Fort Laramie, in present-day Wyoming, as it appeared to a contemporary artist in 1842.

Also, by this time word had filtered back about land-marks and "mileposts" to look for. At the strange rock formations called Chimney Rock and Scotts Bluff in present-day western Nebraska, one-third of the journey would be over. Only 50 miles farther on was Fort Laramie. Just past the fort was Register Cliff, soft sandstone where the emigrants could carve their names as they could later on at Independence Rock—probably 10 or 12 days beyond Fort Laramie. By now cautious emigrants knew that they should try to reach Independence Rock by July 4. It was a good place to celebrate Independence Day, the nation's birthday; but more important, it would mean that they were making good time. If nothing went wrong from then on, they would certainly be in the Willamette Valley before winter.

Elijah White's company came close to reaching that goal. On July 3 they arrived at Fort Laramie, where Dr. White hired Thomas Fitzpatrick as a guide. A few days later, the company came to Independence Rock—and ran into trouble. After a short rest, most of the company moved on. But two men—L.W. Hastings and A.L. Lovejoy—stayed behind to sign the rock. As the two began carving their names, several hundred Sioux warriors suddenly appeared and took them prisoner.

The Indian Encounters

Some west-bound pioneers never saw Indians. Many of those who did found the Native Americans helpful at first. Those in the West offered food for trade, such as salmon, vegetables, and fruit, and served as guides. Indians, who were strong swimmers, helped pilot wagons across dangerous river crossings and herded frightened cattle across rivers.

But many of those same friendly Indians grew angry as increasing numbers of emigrants and their herds of livestock trespassed onto the Native Americans' land, killing the game and the buffalo that the Indians depended on for their very existence. However, relatively few emigrants died at the hands of Native Americans. Far more died from accidents, disease, or infection.

People in an emigrant train defend themselves against an attack by Native Americans.

The Sioux held the men for two hours. Meanwhile, Fitzpatrick waited. When the Indians finally rode toward him, Fitzpatrick went forward to meet them. Using Indian sign language, he made signs of peace. They ignored the signs as they approached closer. Anxious to avoid a fight Fitzpatrick repeated his message that the white people came in peace. Then when the Sioux were almost within gunshot, they suddenly stopped and released the two prisoners.

Elijah White's company encountered no other serious difficulties along the way, and by late fall they did reach the Willamette Valley. But the company had been forced to split into smaller groups, and about half of the emigrants had to abandon their wagons and finish the journey with pack animals.

A year later, in 1843, a much larger emigrant company went west. This was the beginning of the Great Migration, when thousands of emigrants would be heading west. Marcus Whitman had promoted the 1843 emigration, hiring William Sublette as his guide. In the company were nearly 1,000 people with 120 wagons and 5,000 head of livestock. It was not long before trouble began. The emigrants fought over campsites and

A Mormon Trail gravestone marks the burial place of Rebecca Winters, who died of cholera in 1852.

woodpiles. They found they had been following the Santa Fe Trail by mistake, and had to veer sharply to the northwest to get back on the Emigrant Road to the Oregon Country.

Their troubles mounted. They had to plow through drenching rains. Some people gave up and turned back. The draft oxen grew lame. A child fell under the wagon wheels and was crushed to death. A man drowned helping to push a cow herd across a river. Three more people drowned, swept off a raft they had built to float their wagon part of the way down the Columbia River.

As the weary and disheartened emigrants neared the end of this unhappy journey, a rescue party of settlers from the Willamette Valley rushed to their aid. The rescue party guided them the rest of the way.

In 1844, the Great Migration continued as 1,400 more pioneers went west. Some headed for the Willamette Valley, and some for California. This time, the California-bound emigrants were able to make it all the way to Sutter's Fort. This group rediscovered an old trappers' trail from the 1820s that saved them 85 miles of travel. Called Sublette's Cutoff, it cut away from the Emigrant Road beyond South Pass and rejoined it at Soda Springs. Then the route continued to Fort Hall before swinging south toward California.

Since Sublette's Cutoff saved a week of travel, after 1844 many emigrants took it. Others did not, since they would have to travel 50 miles across a barren, dry stretch called Little Colorado Desert. For slow-moving wagons, that could mean from three to four days without a fresh water source for the travelers or their animals. The cutoff began just past South Pass at a place the emigrants called Parting of the Ways near the Big Sandy River.

These impressive mountains at Bozeman Pass, Montana, were named for Jim Bridger.

Emigrants who chose Sublette's Cutoff usually took a long rest in the lush meadows beside the Green River once they had crossed Little Colorado Desert. This allowed their cattle, horses, and oxen a chance to drink and feed, and it gave the emigrants a chance to carve their names on Names Hill, a long sandstone cliff along the west bank of the Green River.

Those who did not take the cutoff were able to stop at the trading post that mountain man Jim Bridger had built in 1843 on Black's Fork of the Green River. This post was located on the main trail halfway between Fort Laramie and Fort Hall. At the trading post was a blacksmith shop, and Bridger even provided fresh oxen—for a price. He traded these for the emigrants' exhausted animals, which he put to pasture in the meadow behind the post. The next year he could trade these rested oxen to other groups of emigrants with worn-out teams.

In 1845, west-bound emigrants numbered 3,000. Once a usable trail to California had been established many more emigrants started going there. Now the Emigrant Road was also known as the Oregon and California Trail. Each year as people headed west in greater numbers, they were learning more about what lay ahead—the best routes to follow and the hazards to expect. They knew they should be prepared for the wooden wagon wheels to shrink in the dry air causing the iron tires to loosen or roll off. And since breakdowns happened, it was better to pack spare axles than heavy cookstoves or wooden bedsteads. From wagon to wagon and camp to camp, rumors and words of advice spread.

As for getting lost, by 1846 the Emigrant Road was so well used that travelers to California or the Oregon Country had no trouble finding their way as long as they did not take a new or untried shortcut. Since wagons

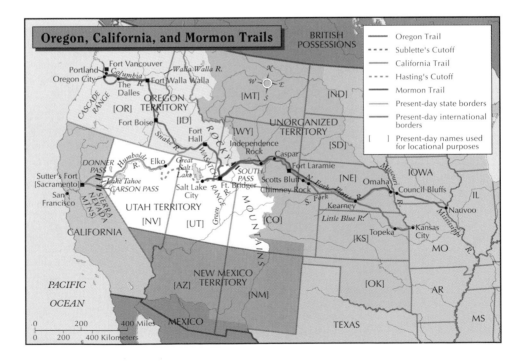

The Oregon, California, and Mormon Trails opened the west to thousands of pioneers hoping to find land and to settle.

sometimes traveled in wide columns hundreds of yards apart, the trail they followed was often a series of tracks rather than a single set of tracks, with changes and short-cuts being added each year.

By 1846, when pioneers reached a settlement called The Dalles on the Columbia River, they no longer had to float downstream on rafts. Instead, they could take the steep and rocky Barlow Road into the Willamette Valley. There were new "jumping off" places such as Saint Joseph and Westport in Missouri. Emigrants also left from Council Bluffs, and traveled along the north side of the Platte River during the first part of their journey.

Manifest Destiny was the term that both the U.S. government and its citizens used to justify their settling in the Oregon Country and California—which did not actually belong to the United States at the time. According to the

"The Way of the Empire Is Going Westward" by a German artist, Emanuel Gottlieb Leutze, expresses the appeal of the Manifest Destiny theory felt by many Americans in their quest to move west.

Manifest Destiny theory, it was the duty and right of the United States to extend its territory westward over the entire North American continent. The term came from a New York newspaper editorial of December 27, 1845, which declared that the nation's manifest destiny was "to overspread and to possess" the whole continent, to develop liberty and self-government to all.

Even after California became a part of the United States, no treaties had been ratified concerning the sale of Native Americans' land to Americans in the Oregon Country. In spite of this, the U.S. government encouraged emigrants to go west to settle there and even offered free land—one square mile of land to a homesteading husband and wife. And in 1848 The Oregon Country was organized into a Territory in preparation for being divided into states.

In 1846 the historian Francis Parkman had come to Westport, near Independence, Missouri, to spend the summer having adventures in the wilderness. He traveled only as far as Fort Laramie with a company heading west on the Emigrant Road. Parkman spent the rest of his summer exploring the area around Fort Laramie and then made a wide loop back to Missouri by way of Bent's Fort in what is now southeastern Colorado, and the northern part of the Santa Fe Trail.

Parkman published the story of his adventures in serial form in magazines in 1847, and as a book titled *The California and Oregon Trail* in 1849. Soon the route once known as the Emigrant Road, and then somewhat later the Oregon and California Trail, came to be commonly called the Oregon Trail.

SIX

The California Trail

In 1842, the year after Joseph Chiles traveled with the Bidwell-Bartleson company to California, he and several other men from the original group returned east by horseback. By then, Chiles figured he had a better idea of what—and what not—to do, and so he decided to lead another emigrant party to California.

Chiles and his comrades began their trek to the East from Sutter's Fort in northern California. The men rode south to Tejon Pass, about 70 miles south of Walker's Pass and about 70 miles north of Los Angeles. From here, they rode north along the east side of the Sierra Nevada. After they reached the Humboldt River, they followed it northeast as far as they could, then continued north along Mary's River to what is now the Nevada-Idaho border. From there they swung over to Fort Hall, where four of the men decided not to go any farther.

So leaving them behind, Chiles and the others took the Emigrant Road east to the Green River. There they learned that Sioux war bands were in the area, so they gave up their plan to stay on the Emigrant Road and decided to go to Missouri by way of Santa Fe. To do this, they followed mountain men's trails through what are now southwest Wyoming and western Colorado until they found the Old

Spanish Road. North of Santa Fe they picked up the Santa Fe Trail and took it back to Missouri, arriving about six months after they left Sutter's Fort.

The following year, west of Independence, Missouri, a standard jumping-off place for going west, Chiles found a group of emigrants who wanted to go to California. They included two daughters of one of Chiles's friends in California, the husband and children of one of the daughters, another family of a husband and wife and three young daughters, and a dozen single men. The emigrants' eight mule-drawn wagons were loaded with furniture, farming utensils, and machinery.

Chiles organized his company and left at the end of May, when he was confident there would be plenty of tall prairie grass to provide forage for the cattle and horses. Chiles left at the same time as John Frémont, who was setting off on another mapping and surveying expedition. It was on that expedition that Frémont would give the name "Great Basin" to the arid region between the Wasatch Range in Utah and the Sierra Nevada Mountains in California.

For a time, Frémont's party and the emigrant company led by Joseph Chiles traveled close together, and Chiles shared with Frémont the wild turkeys and deer he and a friend had shot. After parting from Frémont, Chiles followed the Emigrant Road to Fort Laramie, where he met the trapper and scout Joseph Walker. Chiles hired Walker as his guide and continued on to South Pass.

Just beyond the pass, what was now the Chiles-Walker company stopped at the fort that mountain man Jim Bridger was building with his partner, Louis Vasquez. Nearby, members of the company hoped to "make meat," that is, shoot buffalo. Their supply of food was low, because at Independence the emigrants had made the mistake of packing too much heavy machinery and not enough provisions.

Unfortunately, that summer Sioux and Cheyenne raiders had frightened the buffalo away from the area around Bridger's land, so the Chiles-Walker company had to give up on the buffalo hunt and continue to Fort Hall. By this time, the trading post had been bought by Hudson's Bay Company. When the Chiles-Walker company first arrived, the post's English commander refused to sell any beef cattle to the emigrants. Although the commander soon relented, Chiles concluded it might be wiser if he and some of the younger men set off on horseback, living off the land until they got to California. Walker could keep most of the food and stay with the wagons and look after the rest of the company, including all the women and children.

So Chiles and the other horsemen rode on to Fort Boise. There they left the main trail to follow the Malheur River across what is now the southeastern corner of Oregon. As they continued south, game was hard to find and they nearly starved before they finally reached Sutter's Fort in early November.

Meanwhile Joseph Walker left Fort Hall with the rest of the party and the wagons. He took a trapper's trail to the Raft River. Then, following the Mary and Humboldt Rivers, he worked his way south and west toward the Humboldt Sink. Unable to find a mountain pass he could get over with the wagons, Walker kept moving south along the eastern edge of the Sierra Nevada. At the Owens River near what is now the town of Lone Pine at the base of California's Mount Whitney, the Walker company had to abandon all of the wagons. Now everyone rode, including the women who carried the children or put them in baskets slung over the horses' backs.

Sutter's Find

In 1845 John Sutter, a pioneer trader and landowner, wanted to build a sawmill on the South Fork of the American River in northern California. He hired James Marshall, a carpenter who had traveled west three years earlier, to help him.

In the winter of 1848, Marshall noticed yellow flakes shining in the water. He showed them to Sutter, and both agreed that the flakes were gold! Although they tried to keep Marshall's discovery a secret, the news leaked out and immediately the gold rush was on. From around the world fortune seekers flocked to the California gold country. By 1849 the hills of California were flooded with gold seekers—known as "forty-niners."

After this discovery, the number of people going west mushroomed, and many of them were forty-niners. In April of 1849 alone, more than 20,000 people left for the Oregon Territory and California. To get west, some followed the Santa Fe and Gila Trails to southern California and then went by ship to San Francisco. Others followed the Oregon Trail to where the California Trail branches off.

A group of prospectors hoping to find gold pose by a sluice box in California. The woman has apparently just brought them food in the basket on her arm.

Soon after New Year's Day, two weeks later, the two halves of the Chiles-Walker company were reunited.

So neither Joe Chiles nor Joe Walker had yet found a trail to California that emigrants and their wagons could follow. The first group of California-bound emigrants to succeed in going all the way to California by wagon was the Stevens-Murphy party.

When Martin Murphy decided to move to the Pacific Coast from his Missouri farm in the winter of 1843, he had no way of knowing whether the emigrant train led by Joseph Chiles had ever made it to California. For by winter no rider could have made it across the snow-covered California mountains to let people back east know what happened. And to send a message east from California by ship would take months.

Unsure of the fate of those who had gone before, the widower Murphy still decided to emigrate to the West. In the spring of 1844 Murphy arrived in Council Bluffs on the Missouri River. With him came many family members— two sons and their wives, a married daughter and her husband, eight grandchildren, four of Murphy's unmarried children, and several other Murphy relatives.

The Murphys joined a large company of 40 wagons. There were 23 emigrants altogether, including three experienced mountain men. One of them, Elisha Stevens, was elected the company's captain. About half of the group were going to Oregon City, and the rest to California.

After leaving Council Bluffs, the company continued along the north side of the Platte River—the route followed in 1836 by Marcus Whitman and his fellow missionaries when mountain man Fitzpatrick led them west. This was also the route that the Mormons would later take.

The Stevens-Murphy company reached Independence

Rock soon after the Fourth of July and held a small celebration. After crossing the South Pass they went down to the Little Sandy River. From here, the group headed straight west toward the Green River. Known as Sublette's Cutoff, this route was a popular way for emigrants to shave four or five days of travel off their journey along the Emigrant Road.

From Fort Hall, the Stevens-Murphy company could follow the tracks that Joseph Walker had made the year before, leading to the Humboldt River. From the Humboldt River, the company was able to reach the Humboldt Sink. There an old Indian chief named Truckee gave the party directions to a pass over the Sierras. Some of

Sections of the Truckee River, here shown in winter, are still almost as untamed as they were in the 1840's.

the men rode ahead to scout out the route, then led the wagons across the 40-mile desert to what is now the Truckee River, near today's Reno, Nevada.

Company members left some of their wagons here, to be picked up the next spring. But they kept five of the wagons, and continued up into the Sierra Nevada Mountains. When they came to a granite wall at the base of the mountain pass they had to cross, the emigrants unloaded the five wagons and carried their contents—and also the small children—to the top of the pass. Then, they unhitched the oxen and walked them up a narrow path to the top. After attaching chains to the wagons the men pushed from below and the oxen pulled from above and managed in this way to haul the wagons up the granite wall and onto the mountain pass—now called Donner Pass.

As snow began to fall, the group camped partway down the mountain. But that night, Mrs. Martin Murphy (the elder Murphy's daughter-in-law) gave birth to a baby. So the group decided to leave the five wagons where they were and set up a winter camp for the women. The men butchered most of the cattle, to be left for food, and built a log cabin. Two men stayed to look after the women and children. The others drove the remaining cattle down the mountain, arriving at Sutter's Fort in a few days.

In the spring those at winter camp, including the new baby—Elizabeth Yuba Murphy—were rescued, along with the five wagons. The journey had been difficult, but the Stevens-Murphy company had made it to Sutter's Fort, the first emigrants to take their wagons all the way from Independence to California.

Now, at last, there was a California Trail in addition to the Emigrant Trail to the Oregon Country.

Two years after the Stevens-Murphy group crossed the Sierra Nevadas, another party, led by George and Jacob Donner, was caught by a blizzard in the pass that bears their name. Only 47 of the 82 settlers in the party survived.

SEVEN

Other Trails West

Mormon Trail

Since the founding of the Church of Jesus Christ of the Latter Day Saints by Joseph Smith in 1830, the members known as Mormons had to move many times, driven away by neighbors of different faiths. After being forced to move from New York to Ohio to Missouri, the Mormons finally settled in Nauvoo, Illinois, on the east bank of

In this woodcut, a group of Mormons is shown crossing the plains during a snowstorm.

the Mississippi, in 1839. But even there, these Mormon followers of Joseph Smith were unwelcome. After Smith's death, their new leader, Brigham Young, searched for another place where his people could live in peace.

In 1846 Brigham Young chose a place that is now in the state of Utah. Young was partly influenced by the report of John Frémont, which gave a glowing description of Great Salt Lake and the peaceful area around it.

Mormon emigrants in their covered wagons began to leave Nauvoo in the winter of 1846-47. They crossed the frozen Mississippi River and traveled through Iowa, establishing a winter settlement in the Council Bluffs-Omaha area near the Missouri River. In the summer of 1847, Brigham Young crossed the Missouri with the first company of 14 men, three women, and two children. As they went on west, other companies followed—with several hundred wagons in each train. By the end of 1847, 15,000 Mormons, 3,000 wagons, and 30,000 head of cattle had crossed the Missouri River to what is now Nebraska. Once they started west along the Platte River, the emigrants broke up into smaller groups. But all of them stayed on the trail on the north side of the Platte—across the river from non-Mormon emigrants who were heading west along the trail on the south side of the Platte.

As the Mormons traveled west, the first groups put up signs along the way to guide those who followed. Many planted seeds, so that the bounty of garden vegetables might greet those who came after. This trail they took to their new community in the West was known as the Mormon Trail (see map page 69).

Once the Mormons reached what is now Wyoming, they left the Platte River. From then on, they had to share the Oregon Trail with non-Mormons. After leaving the Platte for the valley of the Sweetwater River, the trail criss-crossed the Sweetwater six times in a three-mile stretch. At the Parting of the Ways, just past South Pass, the Mormons left the regular Oregon Trail and started south toward the Great Salt Lake and their new home in what for a time would be the Territory of Utah.

An artist's depiction of the arrival of Brigham Young (center in top hat) at Great Salt Lake along with Mormon settlers, a Native American, and several mountain men.

Goodale's Cutoff.

This cutoff had once been an Indian trail. It left Fort Hall to wind north and west, through lava rock and sagebrush desert in Idaho, past what is now Craters of the Moon National Monument. The trail joined the regular Oregon Trail at Boise. The cutoff got its name from Tim Goodale,

Pahoehoe Flow in Craters of the Moon National Park.

who in 1862 led a large wagon train of 338 wagons, 820 men, and 1,400 head of livestock over this trail. The wagon train was so large that the emigrants spent about three hours getting in and out of camp each day.

Applegate Trail.

This trail was developed around 1846, after young Oregon settler Jesse Applegate and his brother set out with a dozen friends to find a better wagon road to the Oregon Country. On horseback, the young men rode south from Oregon City, near present-day Portland, through what are

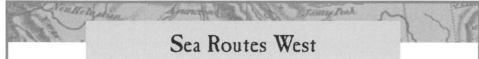

Sea Routes West

Although most emigrant families went west overland between the 1830s and 1860s, there were other ways for easterners to reach Oregon or California.

They could go by ship around the horn (the tip of South America) or they could sail as far as Mexico or the Isthmus of Panama, and then cross over to the Pacific coast and board a ship bound for San Francisco. Going by ship had its drawbacks. It was costly. Going around the horn took a long time, the trip was boring, and the weather was often disagreeable.

now Corvallis, Eugene, Roseburg, Grants Pass, Medford, and Klamath Falls, in Oregon, and continuing to Lassen's Meadows in northern California.

The trail cut across the northeast corner of California and across what is now northern Nevada to Fort Hall. Besides discovering a new way to reach the Oregon Country, the Applegates and their friends added a section to the route of California-bound emigrants.

Hudspeth Cutoff.

Instead of following the Oregon Trail to Fort Hall, after 1849 some California-bound travelers left the Oregon Trail near Soda Springs in today's southeast Idaho to take the Hudspeth Cutoff. This was an old Indian route that more or less paralleled the Snake River, but was 40 miles to the south of the Snake.

Preserving the Trails

While many roads and highways follow closely routes taken by explorers and pioneers, traces of some early trails are not easy to find. Most of these routes are not presently indicated by historical markers or reconstructed areas. Fortunately, this is not always the case. There have always been people interested in preserving our important historical sites for future generations.

Since the Oregon Trail was a series of tracks rather than one single track, in time many of these tracks were plowed by farmers, or built over to put in railroad tracks or to

In 1906 Ezra Meeker set out in this wagon to retrace the route from west to east that he had taken the other way in 1852 to reach Oregon. The record of his efforts during the next few years to preserve the trail was painted on the wagon's canvas.

make roads or highways. By the early 1900s, in Washington State, Ezra Meeker was concerned that the Oregon Trail would disappear completely, and be forgotten. So Meeker, who had come over the trail to settle in the Oregon Territory in 1852, worked to keep the memory of the trail alive. In 1906, at the age of seventy-six, he set out in a covered wagon, retracing the trail from west to east.

He gave public lectures along the way and later met with congressmen and with President Theodore Roosevelt to discuss ways the federal government and individual states could help to preserve this important heritage.

Wagons traveling the Oregon Trail in Wyoming made these ruts which still exist today.

In 1978 Congress designated the Oregon Trail a National Historic Trail and federal, state, and local agencies are working to mark and preserve not only the Oregon Trail, but other trails used by the emigrants. As a result, even today, there are many places where visitors can see the ruts left by the thousands of wagons that went west 150 years ago. Through central Nebraska, parts of Interstate 80 and Highway 26 follow closely the route of the Oregon and Mormon Trails. Federal and state highways through Wyoming, Idaho, and Oregon parallel or cut across much of the Oregon Trail. Emigrant trails in all of these states are well marked.

Glossary

battalion A large number of organized soldiers.

botanist One who specializes in the scientific study of plants.

buffalo grass Thick grass native to the plains of central North America.

bullwhacker Driver of oxen teams.

camino real Spanish for "king's road," or "royal roads."

caravan Group of people with wagons or pack animals traveling together.

cavalry patrol Army troops on horseback for security or observation purposes.

Conestoga wagon Covered wagon with broad wheels used by freighters and pioneers; named for Pennsylvania town where wagons were built.

Continental Divide Mountain ridges from Alaska to Mexico that divide river systems: rivers east of the Divide flow toward the Mississippi River and those west of the Divide flow toward the Pacific Ocean.

emigrant One who leaves one region to settle in another; in American history, a pioneer who moves westward.

Emigrant Road Early name for Oregon Trail.

fiesta Festival or party, from the Spanish *fiesta*.

ford Cross a river or other body of water where it is shallow enough to walk or ride an animal; that part of the body of water where this is possible.

freighter One who hauled freight by mule train or ox-drawn wagons.

geyser Natural hot spring that spouts water and steam from time to time.

Great Migration or Great Western Migration Term for the mass of easterners who headed west to settle in the mid-1800s.

homesteader One who acquired a piece of public land by settling and farming it for five years, according to the Homestead Act of 1862.

keelboat Riverboat with keel but no sails; moved by poling, rowing, or towing; used to haul freight.

Louisiana Purchase Area from Mississippi River to Rocky Mountains and from Canada to Gulf of Mexico, bought from France by Thomas Jefferson in 1803 for $15 million; explored by Lewis and Clark from 1804 to 1806.

"make meat" Mountain man and trapper term for "shoot buffalo."

manifest destiny A belief, held mainly in the 1840s, that the U.S. should, and was meant to, expand its territory to include as much of North America as possible.

mountain men Hunters and trappers in the Rocky Mountains who explored the West in early 1800s; they included Jim Bridger, Robert Campbell, Jedediah Smith, William Sublette, and Thomas Fitzpatrick.

muleskinner Driver of mule teams.

Northwest Passage Nonexistent water route from the Atlantic to the Pacific across North America, sought by navigators since the 1500s.

Oregon Country Area from California border to Alaska, and from the Pacific Ocean to the Rocky Mountains, held jointly by United States and Great Britain from 1818 to 1846.

Oregon Territory United States territory created in 1848 that included all of present-day Washington and Oregon.

Oregon Trail Originally a trappers' trail; followed by westbound emigrants especially in the 1800s and first known as the Emigrant Trail and then the Oregon and California Trail.

ornithologist One who makes a scientific study of birds.

pass Gap or low place in a mountain range with room for people and animals to go through.

plew Name mountain men gave to beaver fur.

prospector One who explores an area for mineral deposits.

province A division of a country; an area or district similar to a state.

rendezvous Yearly get-together of trappers and traders in Rocky Mountains in mid-1800s for exchange of furs for supplies.

scout Person sent ahead by a group to gather information, such as hazards on the trail or good places to camp.

sink Natural depression in land surface.

skin lodge Shelter made of buffalo hides draped over poles, used by certain Native American groups.

source Place where a river or stream "rises," or begins.

spring Stream of water that flows naturally from the earth.

surveyor One who uses special equipment to measure size, length, width, and elevations of land areas, frequently to determine boundaries.

turquoise Bluish-green mineral prized as gemstone when polished.

Warner's Ranch Ranch in southern part of Upper California owned by an American who adopted Spanish ways and took the name Juan José Warner; it was a popular stop for trappers and traders in the 1830s.

Further Reading

Bentley, Judith. *Explorers, Guides, and Trappers.* 21st Century Books, 1994

Bidwell, John, et. al. *First Three Wagon Trains.* Binford and Mort, 1993

Blegen, Melvin and Blegen, Daniel. *Bent's Fort: Crossroads of Cultures on the Santa Fe Trail.* Millbrook, 1995

Collins, Jim. *Settling the American West.* Franklin Watts, 1993

Dailey, Arther and Dailey, Pamela. *The Gold Rush of 1849: Staking a Claim in California.* Millbrook, 1995

Emsden, Katherine N. *Voices from the West: Life Along the Trail.* Discovery Enterprises, 1992

Fisher, Leonard Everett. *Oregon Trail.* Holiday House, 1990

Greenberg, Judith E. and McKeever, Helen Carey. *A Pioneer Woman's Memoir.* Franklin Watts, 1995

Hatch, Lynda. *Oregon Trail.* Good Apple, 1994

Katz, William. *The Black West.* Open Hand, 1987

———— *Black Women of the Old West.* Atheneum, 1995

———— *The Westward Movement and Abolitionism.* Raintree Steck-Vaughn, 1992

Lake, A.L. *Women of the West.* Rourke, 1990

Lavender, David. *The Santa Fe Trail.* Holiday House, 1995

Shellenberger, Robert. *Wagons West: Trail Tales—1848.* Heritage West, 1991

Smith, Carter, ed. *Exploring the Frontier: A Sourcebook on the American West.* Millbrook, 1992

Upton, H. *Trailblazers.* Rourke, 1992

Van der Linde, Laurel. *The Pony Express.* Macmillan, 1993

Van Leeuwen, Jean. *Bound for Oregon.* Dial Young Books, 1994

Bibliography

*Indicates book of special interest to young adult readers

Block, Jr., Louis M. *Overland to California in 1859*. Cleveland: Block Co., 1984.

Cleland, Robert Glass. *From Wilderness to Empire, A History of California, 1542–1900*. New York: Alfred A. Knopf, 1944.

*Fisher, Leonard Everett. *The Oregon Trail*. New York: Holiday House, 1990.

Gilbert, Bill. *The Trailblazers* ("The Old West" series). New York: Time Life Books, 1973.

Goetzmann, William H. *Exploration & Empire*. New York: W.W. Norton Co., 1978.

Grant, Bruce. *Famous American Trails*. Chicago: Rand McNally & Co., 1971.

Hafen, LeRoy. *Broken Hand*: *The Life of Thomas Fitzpatrick, Mountain Man, Guide and Indian Agent*. Lincoln: University of Nebraska Press, 1981.

_____*Mountain Men and Fur Traders of the Far West*. Lincoln: University of Nebraska Press, 1982.

Hafen, LeRoy and Ann W. *Old Spanish Trail*. Glendale, California: The Arthur H. Clark Company, 1954.

*Hillman, Martin. *Bridging a Continent. (Encyclopedia of Discovery and Exploration, vol. 8)*. London: Aldus, 1971.

Hulbert, Archer Butler, ed. *The Call of the Columbia (Overland to the Pacific, vol. 4)*. Denver: The Stewart Commission of Colorado College and the Denver Public Library, 1934.

Lavender, David. *The Overland Migrations*. Washington, D.C.: Division of Publications, National Park Service, n.d.

_____*Westward Vision, The Story of the Oregon Trail*. New York: McGraw-Hill, 1963.

Magoffin, Susan Shelby, (Stella M. Drumm, editor). *Down the Santa Fe Trail and Into Mexico, The Diary of Susan Shelby Magoffin 1846–47*. New Haven: Yale University Press, 1962.

Maxey, Chester Collins. *Marcus Whitman—his Courage, his Deeds, and his College*. New York: The Newcomen Society in North America, 1950.

Monaghan, Jay. *The Book of the American West*. New York: Bonanza Books, 1963.

_____*The Overland Trail* ("The American Trail" series). Indianapolis: The Bobbs Merrill Company, 1947.

Morgan, Dale, ed. *Overland in 1846: Diaries and Letters of the California–Oregon Trail*. Georgetown, California: The Talisman Press, 1963.

Morison, Samuel Eliot. *The Oxford History of the American People*. New York: Oxford University Press, 1965.

Murphy, Virginia Reed. *Across the Plains in the Donner Party, a Personal Narrative of the Overland Trip to California, 1846–47*. Golden, Colorado: Outbooks, 1980.

*National Geographic Editors. *Trails West*. Washington, D.C.: National Geographic Society, 1979.

Ormsby, Waterman L. (Only Through Passenger on the First Westbound Stage). *The Butterfield Overland Mail* (Edited by L.H. Wright and J.M. Bynum). San Marino, California: The Huntington Library, 1960.

Page, Elizabeth. *Wagon's West*. New York: Farrar & Rinehart, Inc., 1930.

Parkman, Francis. *The Oregon Trail* (edited by E. N. Feltskog). Madison: The University of Wisconsin Press, 1969.

Patton, Phil. *Open Road*. New York: Simon & Schuster, 1986.

Pindell, Terry. *Making Tracks*. Weidenfeld, New York: Grove, 1990.

Place, Martin T. *Westward on the Oregon Trail*. New York: American Heritage Publishing Co., 1962.

Sandoz, Mari. *The Beaver Men.* Lincoln: University of Nebraska Press, 1978.

Santa Fe Trail (by the editors of Look). New York: Random House, 1946.

Schlissel, Lillian. *Women's Diaries of the Westward Journey*. New York: Schocken Books, 1982.

Simmons, Marc. *Following the Santa Fe Trail: A Guide for Modern Travellers*. Santa Fe, New Mexico: Ancient City Press, 1984.

Sprague, Marshall. *The Mountain States*. New York: Time Life Books, 1967.

Stegner, Wallace. *The Gathering of Zion, the Story of the Mormon Trail*. New York: McGraw-Hill, 1964.

*Stewart, George R. *The California Trail, an Epic with Many Heroes*. New York: McGraw-Hill, 1964.

*Time Life. *The Pioneers* ("The Old West" series). New York: Time Life Books, 1974.

U.S. Department of the Interior, Bureau of Land Management. *A Step at a Time: The Oregon Trail*. Idaho, Oregon & Washington Offices of Bureau of Land Management, May, 1993 (pamphlet).

Vestal, Stanley. *The Missouri* ("The Rivers of America" series). New York: Farrar & Rinehart, Inc., 1945.

*Viola, Herman J. *Exploring the West*. Washington, D.C.: Smithsonian Books, 1987.

Waitley, Douglas. *Roads of Destiny, The Trails that Shaped a Nation*. Washington, D.C.: Robert E. Luce, Inc.

Wheeler, Keith. *The Scouts* ("The Old West" series), Alexandria, Virginia: Time Life Books, 1978.

White, Syewart Edward. *The FortyNiners (Chronicles of America, vol. 25)*. New Haven: Yale University Press, 1918.

Winther, Oscar Osburn. *Via Western Express & Stagecoach*. Stanford, California: Stanford University Press, 1945.

Index

Note: Page numbers in italics indicate maps; numbers in bold indicate illustrations.